Got Liberty?

Charles C. Heath
Farah Bazzrea
Suzan Dickinson

Proverbial Publishing
125 N. Trade St.
Shelby, NC 28150

Proverbial Publishing

125 N. Trade St.
Shelby, NC 28150

Library of Congress Cataloging in Publication Data

Library of Congress Control Number: 2002108945

Heath, Charles C.
    Got Liberty?/ by Charles C. Heath, Farah Bazzrea, and Suzan Dickinson.

    ISBN 0-9721935-0-2 13.95

Printed in the United States of America.

Dedication

We dedicate this book to the victims of terrorism.

We express our deepest gratitude for those Americans fallen in defense of our liberty. Likewise, we pray to our Lord to comfort the families whom not only have suffered loss, but also those whom have experienced the fear of loss. Also, we salute those Americans whom have risked their lives to support, rescue and aid those fallen. Finally, we commend those Americans that have supported the victims and their families, with expressions of love, patriotism, and financial contributions.

May the ultimate price paid by our fellow Americans, be sufficient to revitalize America, to awaken our patriotic zeal, and to instigate a conservative, political renaissance, resistant to existing political partisanships and hierarchies.

Additionally, we dedicate this book to American parents. It will be your love for your children, which will be the impetus for a political restoration of fiscal responsibility in our nation's government.

God Bless America!

Contents

Foreword

Our intentions are to provide historical evidence, combined with recent events and current issues, to encourage Americans to assess their current personal priorities and values. Then consider the effects of a loss of personal and economic freedoms *upon* those values. The personal price required to protect our liberty will seem a bargain.

Many Americans, awash in the comforts provided by our free society, have relegated the governing of their lives to their political representatives. Unfortunately, many of our nation's politicians, entangled in the political web of lobbyists, special-interest groups, liberal-minded intellectuals and campaign fund-raising, have lost focus of their intended purpose, often ignoring the majority of their constituency's best interests.

Our benevolent government, with all its military might, is unable to defend itself against these liberal agendas assaulting our Constitution, our free enterprise economic system, and our personal freedoms. For the record, our government is not the problem, it is functioning as designed. However, to their detriment, the American citizens have allowed an unmitigated plundering of political favors, granting economic gain to special-interest groups, government contractors, campaign contributors, foreign governments, and politicians, themselves.

We realize this book alone, will not create the necessary change in our nation's thoughts and deeds to suffice. However, we are compelled to contribute to the fostering of candid and essential national discussions. Without a national awareness of the enormous challenges our nation faces in the twenty-first century, Americans will not be forthcoming with solutions. Quoting President Ronald Reagan in his autobiography, *An American Life, Ronald Reagan, The Autobiography*:

> Freedom is the recognition that no single person, no single authority or government has a monopoly on the truth, but that every individual life is infinitely precious, that every one of us put on this world has been put here for a reason and has something to offer...

There has never been a more critical time for Americans to stand together to eradicate the blight of greed, self-dealing, and liberal agendas assaulting our nation, than the present. As the world's leader in personal freedoms, economic strength, and cultural diversity, Americans must tend the flames of liberty as they spread throughout the world, ensuring America serves as a continuing archetypal example for the self-governing of a nation. It is not only ourselves, for whom we must sacrifice our time and effort, but our descendents, as well as, the entire world's population whose hope for a better life is predicated on America's survival.

Got Liberty? attempts to inform Americans of the critical need for their political participation and to loosen the constraints upon their creativity. Americans must free their minds from the onslaught of social-conditioning forces prevalent in our media, our schools, our jobs, and our lives.

Think freely. Contrast the paradigms of freedom present in our society with your own ideals; determine which of those are congruent with our founding father's vision. Become a tireless advocate for liberty in your personal, religious, and business spheres of influence by espousing the eternal truths of personal and economic liberty, upon which our nation was founded.

Our nation's future is dependent upon the individual efforts of millions of Americans, just like you. Join the party! Let's respond to our nation's needs, while our nation needs us. Too often, help is too little, too late. Become a modern American hero! Your children will be proud of your patriotic efforts, and more importantly, you will be preserving their future inheritance.

Acknowledgment

We extend our sincerest gratitude and appreciation
to Candice R. Dickinson for her invaluable contribution.
May the Lord continue to bless her life.

Chapter 1

The Vision

Undoubtedly, during the next century, Americans will witness countless changes within our country and throughout the world. If the American citizens choose, by their continued inaction, to allow our nation to descend into a second-rate world power, our individual liberty will decline, as well. It is vital that Americans receive the wake-up call being sounded by the homeless, the unemployed, the impoverished employed, and the poverty-stricken elderly.

Our nation is struggling with colossal afflictions of over-taxation, political self-serving and aloof disregard for our economic and individual liberties. The American citizens must undertake political action to correct our nation's downward course, if the United States of America is to continue to prosper and maintain its ability to defend our personal and economic freedoms.

Since the founding of our nation, Americans have survived severe hardships, defended our country, and built an economic system, second to none. However, our great nation is precariously balanced on the brink of its demise. If we are to preserve our inheritance for our children and future generations, *"We the People"* must once again, accept our patriotic call-to-duty to defend our nation against an imperceptible attack on its very foundation.

Most Americans are either unaware or choose to ignore the flagrant and widespread abuses of power, which are methodically, *increasing* the size of our federal government, our national debt, and our tax burden, while simultaneously, *decreasing* personal liberties, economic opportunities, and our standard of living. It is time for us, the beneficiaries of our founding father's efforts, to begin installments on our tremendous debt of freedom to our nation.

The American citizens cannot continue ignoring their patriotic responsibilities and expect to continue enjoying the same personal freedoms and economic opportunities that were inherited. If our nation is to survive with our personal liberties intact, we must unite, loose our self-absorbed materialistic obsessions, and contribute reasonable amounts of personal time and effort to protecting our birthright.

Sadly, the symptoms of our ailing society are everywhere, *if* we open our hearts and eyes to see them. If we choose to ignore them, ignore our civil responsibilities, and continue to mindlessly pursue materialism, we will have ignored history, failed our founding fathers, failed to heed a successive number of astute statesmen's warnings, and most importantly, failed our children.

In addition to the shamefully, low political participation levels in this country, the liberal thoughts of a select few citizens are leading uninformed individuals to be an unwitting, destructive force in our great nation. For this reason, we are providing information on the issues within the political realm of society in an attempt to entice those disinterested to become involved, and to simultaneously, enlighten those misinformed.

As mature adults, many of us look back on our lives with regret, due to neglecting the many needs within our society. Quite frankly, we wasted our younger adulthood and its accompanying energy, having taken our liberties for granted and ignoring our patriotic duty. This *blindness* probably occurred from the ignorance of youth, the responsibilities of family life and our misguided belief that as *concerned* citizens, we were fulfilling our patriotic responsibilities, as well.

We encourage our fellow citizens to select their own particular area of concern. Whatever your interests, become involved, whether it is the correct placement of street safety signs, charity fund-raising, beautification of our towns and cities, or volunteering for school activities. In addition to the immense personal satisfaction you will gain through your efforts, you will also become more informed to better find solutions to the problems that affect your local neighborhood, city, state and nation. Instead of complaining, make a difference. That's right. Each one of us *can* and *will* make a valuable contribution, if we become involved, informing ourselves on our local, state and national issues.

Write letters to the editor of your local paper, *speak out* on issues that concern you. Encourage others to speak out also, thus fostering public discussions. Organize a neighborhood committee, discuss community goals, and propose plans for achieving them. Support your local city council, county commissioners, and other public officials, by attending meetings. Inform them of your opinion on pertinent issues. They work for *you*. Advise them of your satisfaction or not: you must not remain silent. If you become politically active, everyone will benefit by your involvement and unique contributions to our society.

Please don't expect your elected representatives to *ask* your opinion. How could any government function, even at local levels, if the elected representatives must seek each and every citizen's opinion on the numerous issues faced daily? Our political system was not designed to function in this manner. A democracy requires that *you*, the individual, participate by informing yourself of the issues. Becoming involved and contributing in your own way, is key towards achieving the desirable outcome.

Who has not overheard someone complaining about political decisions saying, *"I wouldn't have done it that way"*, or *"I can't believe they did that"*? Maybe, it was even you who said this. But, the reality of the situation is that often we aren't informed enough about an issue to make a decision, much less be in a position to criticize someone else's.

Voting Homework

There are numerous ways in which citizens can prepare themselves to vote. Initially, when attending a political meeting, objectively *listen* to the speakers, while assessing the direction of the differing views. Strive to *understand* the concerns, fears, and motivations for each. Afterwards, *research* the issues that interest or may affect you. You don't have to be a politician to understand the issues. At the next meeting, you may want to sign-up to speak, or maybe you would feel more comfortable discussing the matter with your representative. If unable to discuss it at length over the phone, it may be a good idea to contact them beforehand, to advise them of your desire to speak with them prior to the next meeting's commencement. We encourage personal contact, as typically, each will experience a more accurate communication experience during face-to-face discussions.

By becoming an active informed citizen, people will appreciate your eagerness to help and value your contribution of time and effort. The more you become involved, the more credibility as a concerned citizen you will gain, thus gaining influence on the political decisions that affect you. All that is required is common sense, a sincere interest in contributing to the betterment of your own life, as well as, society, and your active participation. So remember, we can sit back, complain, feel sorry for ourselves, let someone else make the effort and lose our liberty, or we can become involved and because of our liberty, improve our society for ourselves and future generations. Our nation can be greatly enhanced by the efforts of people like you.

We must study the issues at hand and learn as much as possible about the candidates in each election. We should not rely on others, whom may be biased toward other candidates or agendas. On each issue, we must seek the facts for ourselves. Responsible media sources, personal conversations with the candidates, town meetings, political rallies, and trustworthy friends are good examples of reliable sources of political information. Yet, you must rely upon your *own* ability to make the correct choice by determining which candidate more closely represents your own values and beliefs.

It is not only *acceptable* to disagree with your friends or neighbors on political candidates, it is your constitutionally-granted privilege! On each candidate, look at their background and observe where their true interests lie. Does their record suggest a positive impact in the areas of church and civil activities? Who are their major supporters? Inquire of their motivation for political office. What specific areas of interest do they feel need the most attention and what is their position on each of these? Have they been, or are they now, actively involved in politics? If so, check out their voting record. If possible, *question* the candidates or their staff about their voting history on issues important to you. Only then, can you objectively compare their choices with your interests and make an informed voting decision.

When we voluntarily fail to take the initiative to do these small tasks, we are literally, taking giant steps toward killing our freedom. There has yet to be a plan developed that is a step-by-step formula that can eliminate this process. Our freedom is not something that can be regimented or forced upon us. The love of liberty is similar to the love offered by our Creator, we must consciously choose to receive it. Liberty is an individual quest; it necessitates action to receive its continued blessings.

To be a political observer is one thing, but to participate in the real issues at hand, is quite another. Not only should we vote in the elections, we should affect the decisions regarding which issues or candidates *make* the ballots. Stand up for your own personal beliefs. This is the genius of our form of government. Each individual acts upon their own beliefs and convictions. Our system of self-governing rule determines which representative is more accurately aligned with the majority of the constituents' positions. Therefore, it is crucial for your voice to be heard. Otherwise, your voice, your needs, and your future are *not* included in this process.

We must speak and act upon the needs of our great nation. Like any discipline, a heartfelt commitment to liberty must be continuously rejuvenated on a daily basis by exercising your patriotic liberties. If we take this task to heart, our society will continue to reap the benefits of liberty for generations to come. The recent terrorist attacks on our nation have spurred a national interest in patriotism. We must not allow this patriotic eagerness to wane without cultivating, educating, and implementing a plan of action to transform this patriotism into a politically-active citizenry.

This is America! One of our nation's greatest strengths is the freedom of unhindered, uncensored speech. However, we must remain cognizant of both, liberal individual and institutional efforts, to discredit or prevent conservative, thought-provoking issues from reaching our nation's psyche.

In general, our mass media has declined to initiate any effort in reforming the destructive, nationally-accepted perspective of politics that encourages the belief that our nation's future is beyond the influence of individual citizens. This is just not so! In the presidential election of 1876, the Republican candidate, Rutherford B. Hayes, lost the popular vote to the Democratic candidate, Samuel J. Tilden. However, the electoral vote was disputed and a special commission declared Hayes the winner by one electoral vote. Also, consider the last presidential election.

According to the Florida Department of State's Division of Elections results, President Bush received 2,911,215 votes in the regular election, while Vice-President Gore received 2,911,417 votes on election day. However, the Federal Overseas Absentees vote that was recorded on November 17, 2000, indicates 1,575 votes for President Bush and 836 votes for Vice-President Gore, resulting in a Bush victory by 537 votes. Nearly 300 million citizens in our nation today, and our presidential election is decided by a mere, few hundred voters!

Encourage your entire family to take an active role in political issues. Take your family to the local library and assign each family member a different issue to research for a later discussion at home. This simple family activity will impart the importance of politics to your children at an early age. By developing this interest, they will have a better understanding of the political process and be more prepared to participate in future elections and the governing of their lives. Never forget, by our founding fathers' design, we are an essential part of the political process.

Organize your family, friends, and neighbors with a common vision to promote wholesome moral issues. You may be surprised how many citizens share your same views and await an opportunity to express themselves. Many are waiting on a grassroots advocate, a potential candidate with credibility, vision and a strong ethical background to actively participate in the political process on their behalf.

Because of the inherent advantage given to incumbent politicians, the complicated process of removing undesirable representatives from political office requires many volunteers. People are required for organizing and working campaign offices, distributing flyers and posters, soliciting contributions, polling the electorate for public opinion, and many other crucial tasks. These people should have integrity and a good knowledge of the issues and candidates.

Many people starting out in politics are unaware of the opportunities. There is organizational assistance and general support within each political party. For those not engaged in a major political party, there is The Conservative Caucus, Inc., 450 E. Maple Ave., Vienna, VA 22180. They are also available on the Internet, via their website:

www.conservativeusa.org

The general purpose of The Conservative Caucus (TCC) is to organize America's conservative majority at the congressional district level and to mobilize their resources and energies into political action. The local district caucus represents the broadcast conservative base and rallies around political issues, primarily within its district, informing the voters on issues and soliciting support for conservative candidates and causes.

Another desire of TCC is to signal local sentiment to the elected representatives and counteract the influence of special-interest groups, mostly based in Washington, DC. Organizations like TCC, remind Americans that we are the leaders of this nation. Our elected representatives are empowered with only *that* authority granted them by the American citizens.

Additionally, for those desiring to better understand the relationship between government, our free enterprise economic system, and our personal freedoms, an educational organization, The Foundation for Economic Education, 30 South Broadway, Irvington-on-Hudson, NY 10533, or their website:

www.fee.org

provides an abundance of accurate information on the dynamics of a free enterprise system within a free society.

19

Chapter 2
Begin With Education

To save our nation, we must temper the pursuit of worldly goals in our public schools and return the principles of the Ten Commandments to the classroom. Our nation's obsession with the pursuit of materialism invokes the least desirable human traits within ourselves. America's classrooms must promote a balanced approach to a successful existence, a combination of spiritual morality and humanistic goals.

The *Holy Bible* should be required reading for every high school student in America, as a prerequisite for graduation. Abraham Lincoln stated:

> *I believe the Bible is the best gift God has ever given to Man.*

While Patrick Henry is credited with:

> *The Bible is worth all other books which have ever been printed.*

Noted scholar, Daniel Webster had a clear vision of the importance of the Bible:

> *If there is anything in my thoughts or style to commend, the credit is due to my parents for instilling in me an early love of the Scriptures. If we abide by the principles taught in the Bible, our country will go on prospering and to prosper, but if we and our posterity neglect its instructions and authority, no man can tell how sudden a catastrophe may overwhelm us and bury all our glory in profound obscurity.*

Lastly, John Quincy Adams endorsed this wonderful gift:

So great is my veneration for the Bible that the earlier my children begin to read it the more confident will be my hope that they will prove useful citizens of their country and respectable members of society. I have for many years made it a practice to read the Bible once every year.

The wisdom contained within the Bible, totally independent of an individual's religious beliefs, or lack thereof, must not be ignored due to the possibility of offending a small minority concerned with the possibility that their children may be exposed to religious ideologies. How can the historical records of some of the greatest men in history, the wisdom of Proverbs, the inspiration of Psalms, and the morality and genius of Jesus the Christ, negatively affect our children in contrast to the television shows and advertisements, movies, music, and videos bombarding them daily?

We must choose to set positive examples for our family, friends, and society, as a whole. By demanding that morality be introduced into our schools, we are standing firmly upon the same values that founded our country. Are we ashamed this country was founded under the belief in God and the inalienable rights that are Divine gifts to all mankind? Our national currency bears the motto, *In God We Trust*; is that no longer the truth? Are those hollow words from an estranged past? If we are to take a stand to stop immorality and the epidemic crime and drug-abuse facing our nation, we must educate our children with the greatest guide to a moral and purposeful life available to mankind, the *Holy Bible.*

Yet, *our* government, the same government that was founded upon God's Holy Word, has forbidden His Word to be taught *our* children in *our* public schools. Certainly churches and parents teach America's children the Word of God, but unfortunately, many children and we dare say the majority of those with emotional and sociological problems, do not attend, or are not correctly instructed in the benefits of this wisdom. Many children are graduating without any practical knowledge or ability to apply moral and ethical values in their decision-making processes. Their *end justifies the means* approach to life does not serve them or society well.

According to the May 23, 2002 issue of *The Mountain Times*, the Watauga County, North Carolina County Commissioners passed a resolution putting prayer back in the Watauga County schools. Their courageous resolution was patterned after the Washington County, Pennsylvania measure supporting a similar national initiative in the U.S. Congress that would return prayer in all public schools. The Watauga County resolution states:

> *Whereas, our Country was founded on the precepts of freedom, liberty, diversity and the right of people to acknowledge God to the dictates of conscience; and*
> *Whereas, neither the United States nor any State shall establish any official religion, but the people's right to pray and to recognize their religious beliefs, heritage and traditions on public property, including schools, shall not be infringed; and*
> *Whereas, the United States and the States shall not compose school prayers, nor require any person to join in prayer or other religious activity; and*
> *Whereas, THE Watauga County Board of Commissioners urges all cities and counties across the United States to join in an effort to reinstate prayer in the public schools by passing similar resolutions and uniting in a "Grass Roots" movement for that purpose; and*
> *NOW, THEREFORE, BE IT RESOLVED that the Watauga County Board of Commissioners strongly supports House Joint Resolution 81 introduced in the 107th Congress...*

These patriotic county commissioners exhibited the type of self-determining character, which our nation so desperately needs. Acting upon their constituents' wishes, selflessly exposing themselves to criticism and political uncertainty, these modern-day heroes expound the virtues of Divine guidance in our children's lives. Their conviction to promote the causes of liberty, moral and ethical values, and a spiritually-fulfilling pursuit of knowledge, is exemplary.

As an example of the hypocrisy our government exhibits in reference to education, the recent events in Afghanistan prompted our federal government to purchase ten million textbooks for the Afghan children's education. However, the most significant aspect of this action was the expenditure of the United States taxpayers' monies on educational material containing *Islamic religious* instruction. The federal agency spokesman defended the action by stating that Afghanistan was primarily a Muslim nation and the teachings of the *Koran* were widely-accepted by their culture.

On Good Friday, March 29, 2002, National Public Radio (NPR) broadcast Bob Howard's report on the United States Agency for International Development's (USAID) involvement with the Afghanistan Ministry of Education. USAID spokesman Andrew Natsios, reported the United States was purchasing ten million Afghanistan school textbooks to replace the textbooks the United States had *previously* supplied during the 1980s and early 1990s.

The previously supplied textbooks had *currently* unacceptable illustrations of weapons and texts, discussing *holy jihads* and other *violent religious fervor.* Those textbooks were supplied to foster resistance for opposing Soviet occupation. The Taliban regime used these former U.S. supplied textbooks during their control of the Afghanistan government.

USAID spokesman Andrew Natsios also reported that USAID hired American-educated Afghanistan university professors and journalists to review the text four times to ensure removal of all violence, and sexual and religious discrimination to assure its political correctness.

When questioned about the involvement of the United States government publishing religious textbooks, USAID spokesman Andrew Natsios responded:

It is not political Islam, it is just traditional Islamic

cultural teachings. It is appropriate in the context of other cultures for us to publish text appropriate to society, traditionally, as long as the principle purpose of the instruction is secular in purpose and the great bulk of the text are being printed are secular subjects with no religious instruction in them at all. We do not publish religious material, but if there is a curriculum that is being published and there is some religious instruction... then we go along.

It is difficult to understand the American taxpayers' responsibility to purchase educational textbooks for foreign countries, especially when schools within our own nation lack ample supplies, but it is *beyond* comprehension how our federal government justifies purchasing educational material containing *ANY* religious instruction for a foreign country, while outlawing the *same* practice in our own country.

Furthermore, since our government supplied the previous texts that Mr. Natsios refers to, *"but if there is a curriculum that is being published and there is some religious instruction... then we go along."* and we are publishing the current text, isn't that typical bureaucratic rhetoric? Of course, our government is going along, since it initiated the original action, in the first place!

Additionally, since our government supplied the previous textbooks, which admittedly, contains *radical Islamic teachings*, but are politically incorrect now, isn't that an admission that our government is responsible for *previous* violations of the Constitution? Doesn't this suggest the United States government's complicity in the current Islamic fanaticism present in the outlawed Taliban regime?

We are not advocating the endorsement of any specific religion by our government or even the toleration of specific religious instruction of any type. However, we fail to understand the difference in literary value between the writings of Plato, Shakespeare, Benjamin Franklin and John Kenneth Galbraith, and the written works of Moses, King Solomon, an imprisoned Paul of Tarsus, and the teachings of Jesus the Christ.

Due to past abusive policies by a medieval, power-hungry church, our nation's founding fathers were wary of an association between our new government and the church. However, the study of these Biblical icons in a nondenominational format, teaching their historical relevance and philosophies independent of church doctrines, does not conflict with the United States Constitution.

Why must our schools *completely* ignore the concepts of morality, spirituality, and the eternal laws of human dignity? We allow liberal viewpoints of modern-day social reformers to influence our children, but cringe at *proven*, conservative, ageless wisdoms observing human nature and admonishing upon the common pitfalls of humanity.

It is unnecessary to *force* students to accept the philosophies of Biblical history as *absolute truths*, no more so, than the works of other historical writers. However, exposing our children to the wisdom and moral knowledge contained within the Bible would certainly be a positive contribution to their education and future. We, as a nation, have overreacted to the original intent of our founding fathers' separation of church and state. By limiting our children's education and removing *all* references to Christian historical figures, spiritual morality and Godly virtues, we are practicing *extremism* and weakening our nation's foundation.

President Grover Cleveland once observed:

> *All must admit that the reception of the teachings of Christ results in the purest patriotism, in the most scrupulous fidelity to public trust, and in the best type of citizenship.*

Our secondary educational system tends to equally constrain spirituality and creativity, while promoting conformity to the current status quo. There is little attempt to intellectually challenge the present-day precepts of our society, which in many cases, are counter to the original principles of our Constitution. Ultimately, the lack of a da Vincian approach to modern problems, will only exacerbate them. According to historian Ellen Schrecker's book, *Academic Freedom: The Historical View*, the academic world has:

sanitized its own teaching and research... essentially eliminated the advocacy of controversial issues from acceptable academic discourse.

Since universities offer a forum for the socialist-minded citizens of our nation, the business community should demand equal instruction on the benefits of the free enterprise system. To be effective, an educational program must be fundamentally direct, stated not in theory and abstractions, but in terms of practical experience and knowledge. It must begin with the basic tenets of freedom and the contrasting new morality, which sanctions the sins of socialism. It must also demonstrate anew that incentive is the basic creator of wealth and that their proportional relationship is integral to the free enterprise system. If either is reduced by government interference, the other is proportionally reduced; thereby weakening this precious and unique economic miracle: our *free enterprise system.*

In addition to the influences of liberal private benefactors, our federal government's Department of Education (ED) exercises excessive influence upon student curriculum. It influences the boundaries of *political correctness* for outspoken or passionate educators through the ED's returning of diluted tax dollars, as a means of funding control.

Furthermore, the Department of Education, through no fault of its own, is an example of a failing federal government's centralized attempt to administer a program, devised for the well-being of its citizens, ultimately wasting billions of taxpayer dollars. Their $32.3 billion budget could have a *profoundly* positive impact upon our nation's schools, if directly applied and locally administered.

To illustrate our argument, according to the General Accounting Office (GAO) report to the 104th Congress's Committee on Government Reform and Oversight:

The Department of Education (ED), created in 1979, is one of the newest and smallest Cabinet-level departments. With an annual appropriation of $32.3 billion, its 4,787 employees have the following missions:

*(1) to provide financial aid for education and
    monitor its use;*
*(2) to fund and pursue education-related research
    and information dissemination;*
*(3) to ensure equal access to education and enforce
    Federal Statutes prohibiting discrimination in
    federally-funded programs and activities;*
*(4) to provide national leadership in identifying
    and focusing attention on major educational
    issues and problems.*

However, the committee found a multitude of problems within the Department of Education, probably less than some federal agencies; but nonetheless, eye-opening issues that clearly demonstrate the politicized nature of a federal bureaucracy's attempt to nationally administer fundamental education to our children. For example:

*ED also continues to have the highest percentage
of political appointees among individual departments. As of September 1995, ED has a ratio of
one political employee for every 33 civil service
employees. The next lowest ratio was at the
Department of Housing and Urban Development
with one political employee for every 100 civil
service employees.*

It is easy to understand how nonelected social and political reformers gain control and influence of our children. It is no coincidence that the federal agency with *three times* more political appointees than any other federal agency, is the one that will most impact our nation's future. It is a widely-held truism, *if you want to change societal behavior and expectations, start with tomorrow's generation.* The upcoming generation is easily influenced due to the absence of cultural and historical relevance.

Another GAO observation contained within the report, revealed the immense difficulties faced by a federal bureaucracy charged with the responsibility for oversight of our children's education:

Fragmentation in the structure and administration of ED's programs hinders the Department in carrying out its missions effectively. This is due, in no small measure, to the piecemeal approach through which the programs have been enacted into law. However, ED has exacerbated the situation by its piecemeal approach to program administration. Programs targeting similar initiatives have sometimes been administered by different offices within ED, creating overlap and coordination problems.

Finally, as a summary of the Department of Education's job performance, according to the Inspector General's report:

The same June 1996 IG (Inspector General) report reiterated a number of core problems... The Department

1) lacks a clear vision of how to best marshal its resources to effectively achieve its mission;

2) has a history that is replete with long-standing management problems that periodically erupted, became the focus of congressional and media attention, and subsequently diverted attention from the policy agendas;

3) lacks continuous, qualified leadership, and has yet to successfully implement all of the fundamental managerial reforms recommended by a joint OMB/ED task force in 1991;

4) has a long-standing practice of filling key technical and policymaking positions with managers who, lack requisite technical qualifications, were ill-equipped to carry out their managerial responsibilities;

5) has management structures and systems that have inadequately supported its major initiatives, such as student aid; and

6) does not adequately recruit, train, or manage its

*human resources to ensure that workers can
accomplish the Department's mission and
implement Secretarial initiatives.*

These are not *our* words, but our federal government's own review and appraisal of the Department of Education. Should we ignore it? If you owned a company with a department that received a review like this, would *you* be concerned? The future of your company, minimally, its profitability would be seriously questioned. There would be few alternatives, other than a change of department management, major company-wide restructuring to integrate functions into other departments, or closure.

However, the very nature of a federal bureaucracy combined with human nature, prevents *anyone* from correctly and efficiently administering this enormous task. It is not ED's leadership, or our political leaders' fault. We have not held them accountable, and they are only human. It is our fault, each of us, the American citizens, for not demanding an end to this doomed bureaucratic effort in conflict with human nature and political reality.

Furthermore, if once again, local school districts were allowed discretionary privileges on the curriculum taught to our children, the different representations of ethnic, religious, and social communities throughout our nation could augment their state's requirements, providing for the perpetuation of regional and ethnic cultural diversity. Our federal officials' attempts to homogenize our different cultural identities by dictating national curriculums and requirements, but not enforcing immigration laws, or supporting English as the national language, is hypocritical, as well as, a self-contradictory effort and another sorrowful waste of the taxpayers' money.

Consider, *if* the Department of Education's $32.3 billion annual appropriation was equally divided by the fifty states, it would increase each state's annual education budget by almost $650 million. If directly applied to teachers' salaries, to either attract or retain our nation's most qualified teachers, competing for professionals in the private sector, and invested in educational technologies for our schools, would a national educational shortfall even exist? If so, it certainly would be a powerful step in the right direction!

It is reported that some primary school teachers are required to pay health care insurance in excess of $700 per month for a family of four, while a married couple without children, over $600 per month. When the meager salaries of educators are considered, this represents an enormous burden upon their households. With national debates on educational issues, why aren't the bureaucrats addressing fundamental issues such as, per student funding, teacher-student ratios, and teacher salaries and benefits?

If we expect federal bureaucrats to eliminate their own jobs or to actually improve education in our nation's schools, we are not being realistic, ourselves. The education solution requires difficult decisions made at state and local levels. It is the nature of government to perpetually grow. Much like a tumor, it is only managed by an external force, either surgically, or medicinally. Do we have the intestinal fortitude to administer the cure?

Presently, the primary accomplishment of the federal Department of Education is the nationwide administration of mandated testing, which preoccupies school administrators' agendas and contributes little to the betterment of our children's education. Considering the annual $32.3 billion is over $100 annually for *every* American alive, if you are a family of five, you are paying $500 per year for the Department of Education's mandated *testing* of your children. Perhaps you are paying your share each year and your children are grown, or you have no children. Obviously, this doesn't include state and local school district's property taxes which fund the *public education* of your community's children.

We *must* speak to our elected representatives, teachers, school board members, clergy, family and friends. There is absolutely no loss of individual liberties, when local influences on curriculum are allowed on *our* children. The federal government is not required to ensure equal access of education to our children. Each state is quite capable of administering the education of their citizens. Ask your governor, state representative, local school board members and teachers, if a federal agency is required to oversee your state's department of education. Also, ask them what percentage of tax dollars sent to Washington DC directly contributes to the education of your children.

It is up to the American citizens to decide if ED's expense is justified. Other than the salaries of almost 4,800 federal bureaucrats, which includes over 1,500 political appointees in Washington, D.C., the American citizens aren't receiving much value for the Department of Education's annual $32.3 billion budget. Of course, if the ED was eliminated, our political leaders would be required to be more creative in their efforts to reward political campaign contributors and supporters, but we're certain there are enough *remaining* federal agencies.

This is our government, our country, and our children. Do we want to let someone else decide what is best for their future, or do we want to regain control of our God-given destiny? Discuss this issue with your local Congress representative and United States Senator. Inform them of your opinion and advise them of your appropriate vote in the upcoming elections.

Every American should recognize and embrace political activism as an essential tool for repairing our educational system. We must defend our Divine right of self-destiny. The twentieth-century's most brilliant mind, Albert Einstein, said:

> *The strength of the Constitution lies entirely in the determination of each citizen to defend it. Only if every single citizen feels duty bound to do his share in this defense are the constitutional rights secure.*

Chapter 3
Politics 101

Since the intended meaning of *liberal* and *conservative* has varied throughout history, depending on a country's ruling government and its citizens' perceptions at the time, in order for us to better communicate our usage of the terms, we thought it important to clarify *our* perspective of the fundamental differences between *modern* American conservative and liberal viewpoints. Although the distinction between conservatives and liberals, and their historical variances in meaning could be the subject of an entirely different book, we will reduce this topic to a few paragraphs.

Essentially, a *conservative* believes the original Constitution, human nature, and the free enterprise system will continue to guide our nation into the future with the prosperity and quality of life that is to date, unsurpassed by any nation. Conservatives understand the Constitution specifically granted limited powers to our federal government, and by default, relegated all unspecified authority to the states. In other words, all other governing should be at the lowest possible level of government.

Conservatives believe decisions should be made at the level of government that is closest to its citizens and is more capable of justly governing with more accountability to its constituents, a *bottom-up* approach, if you will. The nature of conservatives is to *conserve* those values, proven principles, and constitutional powers that enhance individual well-being through the process of free choice and the unhindered freedom to create wealth.

The *liberal* position take a *top-down* approach. Liberals believe the federal government can best cure all of society's injustices and inequalities. They do not rely upon, nor trust the individual's ability to determine their own fate, or to govern their own life. Liberals advocate a select few, through a form of centralized government, dictate social and economic controls at a metaphorically speaking, great distance from their constituents.

Liberals advocate a *unitary* system, in which all power is delegated from a central government, while *conservatives*, conserving our Constitution, advocate a system of *federalism*, which elevates states' rights and individual liberties. Additionally, liberals are inclined to use the power of government to manipulate the free forces of a natural economic system, such as our free enterprise system, by redistributing income and wealth by granting special-interest groups certain privileges at both taxpayer and consumer expense.

However, the great conservative statesman, President Ronald Reagan, in his autobiography, stated his case so eloquently:

> *Government exists for their convenience (the citizens), not the other way around. If they are incapable, as some, would have us believe, of self-government, then where among them do we find people who are capable of governing others?*

A quick reference... *conservatives* choose *proven* principles of human nature and God-given rights and devise a government that coincides with these natural instincts. *Liberals* choose *experimental* efforts to rectify human nature, and attempt to devise a government that in conflict with nature, creates an utopian society. However, all of recorded history supports the conservative position as the correct course of action. There has yet to be a government devised by imperfect humans, capable of creating a perfect world.

Are You A Conservative?

Most Americans agree that the *conservative* approach to our nation's current political and economic challenges is the correct course of action. However, busy with our own lives, often we allow *wolves in sheep's clothing* to deceive us. And rest assured, they *know* they must be deceitful. Liberals implement well-planned strategies for their campaigns, in which, smear tactics, the shell game of which facade contains the *real* person inside, and divert the voter's attention to emotionally-charged issues with meaningless rhetoric, are some of the *tricks* included in their campaign bag.

Also, it should be mentioned that liberal politicians are not restricted to any specific political party and many self-proclaimed, conservative politicians are actually liberals in disguise. Furthermore, many historically conservative politicians promote liberal agendas when self-serving interests are at stake.

It is not constructive to point fingers at the individual culprits, that in the past, have step-by-step, weakened the very foundation of the democratic principles which have brought this nation from its modest beginnings to its present-day status as the world's benefactor. During the Great Depression, World War II, and afterwards, there were well-intending reactionary efforts to equalize the success of all Americans. Instead of following the belief that *equal opportunity* is the responsibility of government, our nation's leaders began a continuous, methodical effort to create *equal results*.

In spite of the natural law of survival, individual differences, which determine the level of success and prosperity of each American, were attempted to be negated and equalized by federal legislation. However, the great expense of this noble, if not naive effort, is being continually added to the already burdensome load the average American taxpayer is expected to shoulder with the excessive, unmanageable surplus debt being shamefully left for our children to pay.

When it comes time to make a decision and cast a vote, ask yourself two questions:

1) Do the principles of individual responsibility, personal freedom and human dignity reflect the most honorable aspirations of mankind?
2) Do these principles represent the truth?

If you answered affirmatively to the previous questions, then you are morally obligated to vote for the conservative candidate. Additionally, you must be aware that rarely will a politician profess to be a liberal. It will require you to investigate the candidates, as we have previously recommended. Do NOT expect a sign on their forehead or a statement in their political ads expounding the virtues of a liberal! In most cases, that would be political suicide! As responsible Americans, we must learn to categorize our candidates, independent of their claims.

Discernment is a learned process, since most of us have a tendency to believe what someone tells us. However, some of the lessons learned in sports, might be applied here. Do you recall your baseball coach telling you, *"Keep your eye on the ball"* or the defensive coordinator's tackling instructions, *"Keep your eye on the numbers on his jersey"*? This was to prevent you from being distracted by *fakes*. These instructions will not fail you in politics, either. Do not be misled by *fakes* or *sideline* distractions, keep your eye on the candidate. Look at their personal life, their track record, their campaign contributors and supporters. This will be much more informative than the words coming out of their mouth or their printed campaign rhetoric.

Patriotism

Patriotism should be exalted to the highest level. We must no longer tolerate self-serving greed by individuals and corporations. Neither should we endure the maligned aspirations of politicians who are either intentionally or unintentionally, influencing and misguiding our society gradually towards a socialist state. If we choose to sit back and let others do *our* job, our society will continue its downward spiral in the battle of morality. When moral and conservative people do nothing, we allow immorality to creep in, only to steal, kill and destroy our great system of government, which was founded *by* the people and *for* the people.

Logically, if the available human pool of potential political candidates is a subset of a greater set of all Americans whom have allowed their morality to lessen, doesn't it follow that the morality of our elected political officials decline, as well? Consequently, our society as a whole, is negatively impacted. Remember, *"It only takes one rotten potato to make the whole basket smell!"* Let us clarify. Our *system* of government is not corrupt. However, to our detriment, our lack of expressed interest and concern have allowed individuals of questionable ability and character to gain access to influential political offices within our society.

One of Dante's famous quotes states:

The hottest places in Hell are reserved for those people who, in moral crisis, do nothing.

The time has long since gone for the apathetic American. There is no room in the community of a free society for patriotic neglect. To gain America's liberty required a monumental effort by our nation's patriots and it will require the same effort to protect and keep it. Our fellow Americans, we cannot allow this irresponsible behavior to continue. It is up to us! Surely, our nation's need for your participation in the political process is apparent. Your family, church, school, community, state, and nation are calling for your contribution of time and effort. Will you answer?

Deep inside, every American desires our nation to be swept by a moral revival. Wouldn't it be nice to walk the streets of any neighborhood, any time of day, and not be fearful for your personal possessions or life? Please think about what you and your family can contribute toward this great and noble endeavor. In order to achieve excellent results, we must stand upon the same Godly principles which our founding fathers stood. They stood on the solid, unchangeable Word of God. This is the reason our great nation has weathered the rampages, thus far.

Our society will always be affected by the constant tugging of secular morality. Therefore, democracy requires each of us to cling and aspire to worthy goals and ideals. Our continued freedom will require impressive individual efforts. It is *our* responsibility, as well as, *every* American's, to stand vigilant for the protection of our freedom. An open mind and compassionate heart are essential for understanding our nation's needs and even *more* courage and commitment to fulfill them. We're confident you will soon recognize our democratic form of government requires its citizens to participate in this greatest experiment of liberty and personal freedoms, if it is to continue.

Standing firm for liberty is morally correct! We must not waver, for truth will stand and history will vindicate us. This has been effectively illustrated in the Bible and throughout the history of many great nations.

Freedom is a God-given trust. Let us accept this enormous responsibility with due reverence. Thomas Paine suggested:

> *Those who expect to reap the blessings of freedom must, like men, undergo the fatigue of supporting it.*

The preservation of freedom must be a continuous struggle for *all* generations. It's birth was threatened and tested in 1776. Thanks to the efforts of men like George Washington, Thomas Jefferson, Ben Franklin and too numerous other patriots to name, our nation was created, and exists today, for each of us to enjoy and prosper under its freedoms.

America's future will be determined by *our* response to the current malignant forces threatening our nation. We hold the golden key of opportunity in our hands, but it will require our dedication and *willingness to act* to save our freedom and preserve it for future generations. Don't allow American history to already have had its greatest moments. Read our country's history books, understand the values that our founding fathers fought to preserve. Share these thoughts and ideals with your friends and family. Conserve our liberty without regard for partisan politics and trivial differences. Unite our country for the common good of all humanity. Instill these values in your children. Guarantee your civil and economic liberties remain for them and future generations. Patriotism, comparable to muscles, will atrophy and fail, if not exercised; therefore, the voice of patriotism must be exercised *daily* in our work, our schools, churches, and civic groups across America.

We are obligated by freedom alone, to promote an understanding of liberty. Our greatest ammunition against socialism, communism, and other forms of ailing governments around the world, is our freedom and accompanying prosperity. You could travel around the world asking the citizens of many nations, *"If you could choose a country in which to live, which nation would you choose?"* The vast majority of those that could *freely* answer would choose *The United States of America.* Would there be a nation capable of carrying the torch of freedom, sharing hope and prosperity throughout the world, if the United States of America is allowed to decline into obscurity?

The time is now for our citizens to proudly wave our flag. Don't be ashamed to place your hand over your heart when *Old Glory* passes. Hold dear the values, freedom and liberties that our flag embodies for our nation. Soldiers that have served our country on foreign soil speak of the great pride and relief they feel at the sight of her.

Let us not forget God's gift to America is freedom. What we do with His gift either praises Him or blasphemes Him; which will you choose? So, let us proudly wave our flags *every* day.

Liberty...

Our liberty came from blood, sweat and tears. Many men and women put aside their fears and bled for the sake of liberty for all mankind. We too, must put away our fears. It is time to extinguish our society's immorality by using sound judgment when selecting our political leaders. To change the downward direction of our society, we must start here and now!

Can you imagine how different the world might be today, if the United States of America had not joined the battle against Nazi and Japanese expansion in World War II? Would you want to even consider the possibility of an entire world led by a dominating, tyrannical, political system of repression, genocide, and economic chaos, with almost a complete absence of human rights and dignity?

We *Got Liberty* through wisdom and courage. In order to keep it, we must use informed judgment to take action, before we *lose* the opportunity to serve as *We the People* in our nation's government.

> *To every thing there is a season and a time to every purpose under the heaven*:
>
> Ecclesiastes 3:1 KJV

Now is the time for mending our great nation. Everyone is familiar with the cliche: *"Timing is everything."* All of us have experienced the wisdom of this simple, but insightful statement. All of our intuitions, our research, our daily observations, cry out: *"Now is the time!"*

Chapter 4
Attempts At Freedom

Since the early days of mankind, there have been governing councils and leaders. However, prior to the patriarchs' acceptance and belief in the one true living God, the God of Truth and Righteousness, the Creator of all things, the leaders of these ancient cultures made decisions based upon superstition, coincidences of nature, and other false signs that controlled the destiny of their followers.

Only in the last couple centuries, has modern society been able to commence unlocking the vast secrets of these past civilizations. In 1799, Napoleon gathered a renowned group of scholars for an expedition down the Nile River in Egypt. During this adventurous expedition, a French officer, M. Boussard, discovered the Rosetta Stone, a black basalt stone, measuring approximately 11 inches thick, 3 feet 9 inches high, and 2 feet 4 inches across with three inscriptions, one above the other.

The inscriptions, in Greek, Egyptian demotic, and ancient Egyptian hieroglyphics, recorded a decree of Ptolemy V, in 200 B.C. A French scholar, named Jean Champollion, had a thorough knowledge of Greek and Egyptian Coptic, the last stage of the Egyptian language, written mainly with Greek letters. After years of work, his knowledge of ancient languages enabled him to finally decipher the Egyptian hieroglyphics, and in 1822, he published a pamphlet, *Lettre a M. Dacier*, detailing his efforts. His publication soon became the definitive translation tool for studying ancient Egyptian inscriptions.

Then, in 1888, halfway between Memphis and Thebes, about four hundred clay tablets, ranging from 2-3 inches wide and 3-9 inches high, with inscriptions on both sides, were discovered. Scientists determined the clay tablets were part of the Royal Archives of Amenhotep III and Amenhotep IV. Written in Babylonian cuneiform script, the tablets contained official correspondence from ancient kings of Palestine and Syria to the two Egyptian Pharaohs.

Additionally, in 1905, Sir Flinder Petrie discovered the earliest alphabetic script known to modern man. In a Semitic temple at Serabit, near the turquoise mines in Sinai, he found ancient Egyptian hieroglyphic inscriptions along with an alphabetic inscription, dating back to around 1800 B.C., almost four hundred years before Moses lived in this same area.

These events opened the door for modern civilization to peer through thousands of years of human development and recorded history to learn the knowledge gained and utilized in ancient societies. There were vast libraries of state documents, including leather documents in the 4th Dynasty, rolls of papyrus and vellum dating back to 2700 B.C., and stone, being the most durable, giving us records as early as 3500 B.C., through tablets and monuments covered with exquisite inscriptions.

Scientists and historians have concluded from the study of these ancient texts, that most of these ancient civilizations had highly-organized, centralized governments with autocratic rule in which, slavery was quite common. Typically, there were an aristocratic elite, living a relatively, luxurious life-style, while the vast majority of citizens lived an impoverished existence. Evidently, few personal freedoms were available to many citizens living under these ancient rulers.

However, around the 15th century B.C., when Abraham and his descendents opened their hearts and minds to the living God, His Word became the foundation for undeniable, personal freedoms. This concept of Divinely-inherited human rights led to the rejection of their enslavement. Around 1300 B.C., after four hundred years of slavery, Moses led the previously enslaved Israelites out of bondage. Using the Lord's Word for guidance, the Jewish patriarchs established a free society that was based upon an irrevocable premise of human equality.

Unfortunately, these people later neglected the

Lord's teachings, became complacent about their responsibilities to ensure their freedoms, and squabbled among themselves for leadership. Consequently, various empires, ranging from the Babylonians, Assyrians, and Egyptians, to their own competing kings, enslaved them. Thus, the first known attempt of humanity to live a life of self-determination, as God had instructed, failed.

Cyrus The Great

Cyrus the Great (580-529 B.C.), after defeating the Persian and Medes tribes of Iran, founded the Persian Empire. He installed tribal nobles as civilian authorities and appointed governors, called Satraps, to represent him in each province. Cyrus delegated authority to the Satraps to independently administer each province, allowing religious freedom and cultural diversity.

Although Cyrus considered himself a liberator, after Babylon fell to his army, he proclaimed himself, King of Babylon. The enslaved Jews celebrated Cyrus's conquest of their captors. A year later, he released over forty-thousand Jews and allowed them to return to their Promised Land to rebuild the Temple that the Babylonians had previously destroyed.

With astonishing insight, Cyrus allowed the institutions of his conquered kingdoms to remain intact. His great respect for individual, cultural and religious freedoms quickly established him as an *innovator of rule* for conquered nations. For example, the conquered Hellenes (Greeks) called him *Lawgiver.*

Cyrus the Great, was the first Archaemenian Emperor of the Archaemenide Period, which extended until Alexander the Great, defeated Darius III at the battle of Issus in approximately 333 B.C. According to *Time-Life Books', The Dazzling Reach of Darius's Imperial Spear*:

> *Suez Canal workers digging 20 miles north of Suez in 1866 came upon fragments of a red granite stele that, whole, had stood nearly 10' tall and measured about 7' across. Startled at finding the monument,*

*the workmen would have been even more surprised
had they been able to read the inscriptions on its
sides, spelled out in Old Persian, Babylonian,
Elamite, and Egyptian. These included an astonishing message repeated in all four languages from
Darius the Great, King of Persia:*
*"I ordered this canal to be dug from the Nile,
which flows in Egypt, to the sea that goes to Persia. This canal was dug out as I commanded," he
boasts on his stele, "and ships went from Egypt
through this canal into Persia as was my desire."
According to Herodotus, the canal was wide
enough for two war galleys to pass each other
under oar. Ships took four days to move from one
end to the other.*

*The empire that Darius acquired and extended,
united western Asia from the Mediterranean to the
Indus Valley under a single ruler, covering an area
almost two million square miles, with some ten
million inhabitants.*

*Other achievements of note of the Archaemenids is
the road built between Susa in southern Iran to
Sardis in Lydia (the Royal Road). Herodotus had
calculated that it took Cyrus three months to move
his army from Susa to Sardis, a journey of some
1700 miles. Cyrus is also reputed to have devised
the first postal system. Xenophon reports that
Cyrus first calculated the distance a horse could
go in one day without being too exhausted, he then
had a series of posting stations built distances of
one horse-day apart, hence ensuring efficient flow
of information between the king and provincial
governors.*

Although the Persian Empire was not a classical self-
ruling nation, Cyrus was esteemed as a benefactor to the
citizens of his vast empire. His citizens prospered under his
government's respect for individual rights and liberties, while

delegating authority to civilian leaders of each region. Relative to the alternative regimes of this period, Cyrus's efforts to establish a peaceful empire were impressive, indeed.

The Roman Republic

The Roman Republic is perhaps the most well-known historical experiment in self-rule. Their laws are the foundation for most of the free world's legal systems, while their civil engineering advances are still serving modern cities, today. From 753 B.C. to 476 A.D., the Roman Republic at its peak, included an expansive territory from the Atlantic Ocean in the west, to the British Isles in the north, along the Mediterranean Sea to the Persian Gulf in the east, and north Africa to the Atlantic Ocean was its southern border.

Although originally ruled by kings, the aristocratic nobles actually established the Roman Republic in 509 B.C. This republic lasted almost five hundred years, which is recorded history's longest surviving, self-ruling nation. Their system of representation was the basic framework for our founding father's design of our Constitution. Their system of checks and balances evolved from an ongoing struggle between the landowners and the poor, taking over two hundred years to develop. As a result, historians regard their system of self-rule, as a model of balanced government.

For instance, their legal system was much more flexible than modern laws. They used a common-sense approach to fairness, combined with a respect for local customs, to determine justice. Roman lawyers developed a general set of legal principles, which were called, *law of nations*, that were applied equally, throughout the empire, as well. Although their justice system was considered equitable, their society *did* allow enslavement of non-Roman citizens. Additionally, religious freedoms were not allowed until 313 A.D., either. In spite of its faults, the Roman Republic was the world's most successful attempt at self-rule, which for its citizens, liberated the human spirit for the pursuit of economic self-expression in literature, fine art, and science.

However, in 27 B.C., after twenty years of violent

civil war, as a result of the growing discontent caused by high unemployment, tax abuse, slavery, and the widening gap between the rich and poor, Augustus Caesar proclaimed himself emperor of the new Roman Empire. As dictator, he retained the Senate and assemblies. However, the emperor with his personal advisors, directed the affairs of state, while appointed civil service employees managed the day-to-day business affairs of the citizens.

The Roman Republic unified an immense region of diverse ethnic groups and cultures. After its demise, the leaders of the Roman Empire, eventually intoxicated with their absolute power, became complacent for the rights of citizens and allowed greed, corruption, and self-serving interests to completely, capture their attention. As a result, the great Roman Empire finally fell to disorganized Germanic tribes in 476 A.D. The Roman Republic, much like the Colosseum, the Forum, the Pantheon, and other architectural wonders, lies in ruin. However, many cultural influences, including architecture, Latin, and its greatest contribution, civil law, remain.

Muhammad

Muhammad (570-632 A.D.), a self-made businessman, began another major attempt to establish individual freedom. Babylon was long forgotten and the original Roman Empire had ceased to exist. Europe, stuck in the barbarism of the Dark Ages, was less influential economically, than Africa, today. Constantinople, surrounded by the thriving cities of Baghdad, Damascus, Antioch, and Alexandria, had become the world trade center.

A barefoot orphan, ragged and hungry, Muhammad worked sixteen to eighteen hours a day, sleeping on the bare ground under the sky. He lacked a formal education, but gained much practical knowledge and experience. He soon became widely known and respected.

Muhammad agreed with Jesus the Christ, that pagan gods are powerless. There is only one true God, the God of Truth and Righteousness, who *judges* mankind, but does not *control* it. Individuals, whom are created in God's own image, are self-controlling and responsible for their own acts. Humanity was created in the likeness of God and therefore, all individuals were created equally, with equal accountability.

Muhammad believed the priests that had assumed societal control over the Jews had violated and misinterpreted the teachings of Abraham and Jesus the Christ. Jesus attacked these same priests' actions and reasserted an ultimate Divine accountability. Jesus encouraged His followers to obey the laws of the land, but explained the limitations to their authority, to which all people must recognize.

By age thirty-five, Muhammad was renown for his ministering to the poor and his outspoken criticism of the wealthy citizens' contemptuous treatment of them. Highly respected for his morality, Muhammad experienced several visions, believed to be the angel Gabriel, whom instructed him to proclaim God's message.

Originally, he disbelieved the Divinity of his visions, but after much encouragement by his wife, Khadija, he began to share his revelations with his family and friends. However, most Meccans ridiculed him and he eventually fled Mecca after his wife died, to the city of Medina in 622 A.D.

Contrastively, the people of Medina accepted his preaching and Muhammad quickly became the leading statesman of both the religious and civic communities. He found moral guidance in the Word, which instructed him in the natural and eternal truths for all mankind. He regulated slavery, banned violence, *except* for self-defense and the cause of Islam, abolished idolatry and outlawed the murder of baby girls.

But, much to Muhammad's confusion, the Christians and Jews failed to accept him as a prophet. Consequently, in his struggles to create a new religion, he changed the direction of prayers from Jerusalem, which was originally chosen because of Jewish tradition, to the city of Mecca, further individuating Islam (Arabic translation for *submission*) from the Jewish and Christian religions. Finally, in 630 A.D., after several years of defending Medina from Meccan attacks, Muhammad gained control of the city of Mecca and converted the Kaaba, the most sacred shrine in Mecca, to a

Moslem mosque.

However, Muhammad died only a couple years later in Medina and was buried in the Prophet's Mosque there. Fortunately, many of his cultural advances continued with the spread of Islam throughout the Arabic nations. Although Muhammad's government fell short of the Roman Republic's self-rule design, his valuable contribution to the advancement of humanity with inalienable human rights for a significant portion of the world's population, is especially, worthy of historical recognition.

The Magna Carta

The self-appointed monarchal and dictatorship forms of government continued to dominate the world's political landscape for the following millennium. However, a documented acknowledgment of innate human rights and personal liberties occurred in 1215 A.D. Essentially, the Magna Carta, the great English Charter of personal and political liberty, obtained from King John, was the first modern-day effort to formally establish non-revocable individual liberties. Although King John did not actually intend to abide by the terms, the constitution guaranteed basic personal rights, prohibited increased taxation without consent of Parliament, granted religious freedom without government interference, and made it clear that the king must obey the law, as well. However, these rights were only granted to the English aristocracy, the landowners. Unfortunately, the average English citizen benefited little more than gaining *due process*, under the law.

Nonetheless, shortly after signing, at the King's request, Pope Innocent III repealed the charter and war immediately broke out between the nobles and the king. After King John's death in 1216, his son King Henry III promised to obey the law. The Magna Carta soon became recognized as the fundamental law of England. Although the charter did not revoke the basic premise of the monarchal claim of Divine right of taxation and rule, as a constitutional check on the King's power, it was utilized by our founding fathers in designing the framework of our Constitution.

The Renaissance

During the period following the collapse of the Roman Empire, until the early thirteenth century, the Saracens were thriving culturally, furthering the social applications of mathematics, medicine, agriculture, astronomy, and other disciplines. On the other hand, the western European cultural advances had been relatively modest. The invention of the water wheel and the wind mill were the most significant innovations during this entire era, generally referred to, as the Middle Ages.

However, a dramatic transformation began to occur in the city-states of Italy. Inventions, such as the printing press, which enabled the masses access to knowledge, the magnetic compass and large sailing ships, which expanded trading partners and exchanges of information, and the invention of a mechanical clock, which for the first time in history, made time a commodity, began improving the lives of Europeans.

The printing press *dramatically* increased the total number of handwritten Guttenberg Bibles in existence, from approximately *sixty* to over *six million* printed copies in less than fifty years. This phenomena introduced the average European to the eternal concepts of liberty. Likewise, cheap paper and pencils allowed the conveyance of these principles to their children, friends and families, making education more commonplace.

Strangely, one of the most significant inventions of the period, was the long-range cannon. This instrument of war became the liberator of the average European. No longer could the previously, impenetrable walls surrounding the city-states, protect the ruling-elite families from their oppressed serfs.

These inventions affected the masses, creating a synergy that simultaneously, freed, enlightened, and motivated the Italians to greater heights. Thus, Italy gave the world such notable explorers as Christopher Columbus, Amerigo Vespucci and Giovanni da Verrazano, artisans like Verrochio, Giotto, Donatello and Masaccio, architects such as, Brunelleschi, who revived ancient Roman architecture and designed the Pazzi Chapel in Florence, and Christian humanists like Desiderius Erasmus, who attacked religious superstition, and too numerous other historically-significant individuals to mention.

The dynamics of capitalism, the personal economic benefit gained from one's own efforts, became a powerful force in the movement for individual and economic liberty. The transfer of economic power from the ruling families to the masses, supported by the very realistic possibility of militia reprisals with the long-range cannon, subdued the resistance of the nobility, to little more than guarded dissatisfaction. Some Italian aristocracy even supported the movement.

Soon, motivated by the rewards of capitalism, the entrepreneurial spirit of the artisans and shopkeepers flourished. And as much as the focus of one's life on materialism is considered negatively, the positive aspects of consumerism can be attributed to the pervasive proliferation of priceless works of art by the Renaissance-period Europeans, which are highly acclaimed and appreciated for their contributions to the modern world. The great artists of the period, such as, Raffaello Santi (Raphael), Michelangelo and Leonardo da Vinci's portrayals of biblical figures and events, not only were astonishingly lifelike, but also inspiration for humanity to achieve its Divinely-granted potential.

However, perhaps the final release of the stifling societal controls exerted by the often-abusive, papal church, such as the *holy wars* and the torturing of *evil* disbelievers, occurred when the black plague swept throughout most of Europe in the fourteenth century. Almost half of the population was annihilated, with no regard for church or royalty. Priests, nobility, and peasants were killed, alike.

The commoners' observation of the inability for the nobles, the church, or its loyal followers, to avert the disease, became the basis for the widespread belief in the concept of all mankind being created equally. Additionally, the study of ancient Greek and Latin languages allowed the Italian scholars to examine these ancient cultures, specifically, their laws and humanism, which contrasted the disciplines of history and human actions with spirituality.

As serfdom collapsed and capitalism expanded throughout the region, a steady movement began organizing larger groups of citizens for the protection and benefit of the common good. Originally, there were roughly 250 city-states in Italy, which gradually merged to form the modern nation we know today. Thus, perhaps the Renaissance, which began in Italy and eventually spread throughout Europe, can be credited with, among other things, a significant, if not critical contribution to the birth of the modern nation-state.

The French Empire

One failed effort to govern an empire, occurred after revolution spread over France in 1789. The French Revolution quickly degenerated into a *Reign of Terror,* in which twenty-thousand people, including France's King Louis XVI, were executed. By 1799, the revolution was nearing completion, and the French people wanted a strong leader to stop the anarchy. A national war hero, General Napoleon Bonaparte, became the most likely candidate.

After establishing peace with Europe, following a sequence of remarkable battle victories and political negotiations, Napoleon was appointed first consul for life by the French people in a constitutional amendment in 1802. Rallied by the French people's desire for independence from the European monarchy, Napoleon pursued efforts to liberate the entire European continent from their grasps. The general also planned the demise of the British royalty's control of the currency system, which he perceived as an unjustified surrendering of France's sovereignty.

The Bank of England, securing their interests with pledges of taxation upon their borrower's subjects, loaned money to the European royal family. Consequently, The Bank of England was granted sole rights to issue currency, and a monopoly on corporate banking. Although the entire list of bank shareholders was not released, King George and the Rothschild family were among them.

Opposing central-banking policies, currency debt and foreign control, a cash-starved Napoleon waged a war against the international bankers' interests, which were defended by the British alliance's military. To raise capital, Napoleon implemented an ingenious strategy to reacquire the Louisiana Territory from Spain. Simultaneously, he negotiated with President Thomas Jefferson to sell the Louisiana Territory, once regained, to the United States of America.

President Jefferson, equally opposed to national debt and a staunch proponent of government's *right* to issue its own currency without borrowing from a central bank, negotiated and closed the most lucrative land deal in American history. With common national political interests, the United States cheerfully paid $15 million to France for the Louisiana Territory, which bolstered Napoleon's military efforts to eliminate British economic influence.

The Bank of England's shareholders, British royalty and aristocracy, loaned war-chest funds to a coalition of European countries, including Austria, Russia, Sweden and Britain, to oppose Napoleon. However, in 1806, he defeated them, consolidating nearly all of Europe under his authority.

In addition to Napoleon being an excellent military strategist, he was a worthy civil administrator. He incorporated some of the freedoms gained in the French Revolution into law codes, such as, religious tolerance and the abolition of feudalism. His centralized government divided France into regions, administering an empire of constitutionally-empowered, free people. He promoted science, the arts, and education, while striving to create an efficient government.

However, his political ambitions to eliminate British trade with the European continent led him to suffer a decisive defeat by a British, Spanish, and Portuguese alliance. The allied victory, financed by the Bank of England, ultimately, resulted in the French Empire's loss of Spain and Portugal.

Additionally, after his embarrassing return from the horrible ravages of an extreme winter in Moscow in 1812, where almost 500,000 of his 600,000 troops succumbed to starvation, freezing temperatures, and Russian advances on a retreating army, Napoleon published his *29th Bulletin,* disclosing his blunder.

The news of this disaster heartened the hostile alliance of European nations that had previously opposed and suffered defeat by Napoleon, to unite again. This time, the allies defeated Napoleon in the Battle of the Nations at Leipzig, Germany, in October 1813. Napoleon retreated to Paris and was later captured in March 1814.

One month later, in April 1814, Napoleon abdicated his throne and was exiled to a Mediterranean island named Alba, off the coast of Italy. He attempted to relinquish the throne to his son; however; the French people refused to acknowledge Napoleon II, as the rightful heir to the French throne. The following February, Napoleon escaped, returned to France, found popular support and tried to establish a peaceful coexistence with the neighboring, distrustful capitalists and allied leaders.

Consequently, during *the hundred days* of his second rule, in an attempt to pacify his detractors, he wrote a new constitution that greatly limited his powers. However, undeterred, allied leaders continued to prepare for battle. Nathan Rothschild, the London resident of the Rothschild family, financed the Duke of Wellington's efforts to prepare an army to defeat the French army.

Napoleon advanced his small army into Belgium to battle the Duke of Wellington, and Prussian Marshal Gebhard von Blucher. It was to be his final battle. Napoleon's army was utterly defeated by the British and Prussian forces at the battle of Waterloo, in Belgium, in June 1815.

Napoleon lived the remainder of his life exiled on St. Helena, a British barren island in the South Atlantic Ocean. He died on May 5,1821 and was buried on the island. However, in 1840, the British and French governments, granting his last wishes, exhumed his remains and buried them at the Eglise du Dome (Church of the Dome) Paris, France.

The European Struggle Continues

The German dictator, Adolph Hitler, rose to political power from a culmination of seemingly unrelated political decisions, over a period of a little more than a decade, in various countries around the world. Additionally, the world's economic situation, the political apathy of disinterested citizens, and the same despicable traits of hatred, greed, and lust for power, that have motivated tyrants throughout history, played a significant role in creating an environment that facilitated yet, another maniacal dictator's rise to power.

In 1914, Europe became the unfortunate host to the first modern conflict ever large enough to be called a world war. The war, known as World War I, involved most of Europe and Russia. After the war was finally over and literally, millions of Russians, Germans and other Europeans had been killed, The Treaty of Versailles imposed harsh penalties on Germany, the war's instigator. However, German reparations, as specified by the treaty, soon fell behind due to the devastating decline in value of the German mark. When the treaty was signed in 1918, it traded at four marks to the dollar. When the war debt amount of 132 billion marks was agreed upon in 1921, the mark traded at approximately seventy-five marks to the dollar. Then, in November 1923, after a disastrous decline in value, the mark traded at a staggering 130 billion marks to the dollar!

Finally, in 1924 new arrangements were made to stabilize the German currency. The negotiated Dawes Plan stipulated German payments of $250 million annually, with much of the money to be borrowed from banks in the United States of America.

However, in 1929, Hitler's party, NSDAP, the National Socialist German Worker's Party, opposed the American banker, Owen Young's new proposal, the Young Plan, that had been worked out to make a final settlement of Germany's reparation bill. By joining with the Nationalist Party in their opposition to this settlement, the Nazis gained new financial support and Hitler was elevated to national prominence.

Meanwhile, a worldwide agricultural overcapacity began a series of global economic calamities. Due to American domestic protectionist measures, imported agricultural products found weak to nonexistent markets in the United States, resulting in the inability of the United States banks to collect their foreign debts from countries attempting to pay war reparations. Additionally, the New York Stock Exchange collapsed, and numerous major banks failed, including the principal Austrian bank, the Credit-Anstalt, and the German bank, the Darmstadter-National.

In spite of a one-year suspension of war reparation payments, this series of events increased the German hardships and ultimately, resulted in a complete failure of further payments. This humiliation for the German government proved to be a political windfall for the Nationalist and Nazi political parties. Due to the existing government's inability to control the mark's decline and the ensuing financial hardships throughout Germany, radical political parties attracted new interest.

After a previous defeat by President Hindenburg in the German presidential election in 1932, Adolph Hitler became chancellor of Germany in January 1933. Adolph Hitler's Nazi party had finally secured control of Germany through an open policy of intimidation, covert terrorist campaigns, and cunning political maneuvers, coinciding with national and global economic hardships.

Within a few months of acquiring the chancellor's office, Hitler established his first concentration camp, Dachau, near Munich. Hitler's Nazi regime soon began a national campaign to rid Europe of all Jews and any other *people* considered inferior to Germany's *master race.*

In November 1936, the Anti-Comintern Pact was signed by Germany, Japan, and later, Italy. The plan was to threaten the Soviet Union from both the east and the west. Two months later, Hitler refuted the Treaty of Versailles. Within six months, the Soviet Union began purging the Soviet Communist Party and thirty-five thousand officers, many top-ranking, were either arrested, executed, or simply disappeared.

In 1939, in spite of a nonaggression pact, Hitler's forces thrust Europe into another world war with the invasion of neighboring Poland. While Hitler was consolidating his power in Germany, Japan was strategically expanding its empire through military conquests in south and central Manchuria with acts of sabotage on the South Manchurian Railroad. Shortly thereafter, the Japanese military began unilateral actions without governmental consultations. Their goal was to create a *Greater East Asia Co-Prosperity Sphere,* an *economic* association of Asian nations under the leadership of Japan. The Japanese Constitution required active-duty, serving military officers as ministers of the army and navy, resulting in the potential collapse of any government that opposed military action. Therefore, the constitutional government, arguably, had no choice, but to concede authority and support the young militant officers' ambitious agenda.

Due to a Chinese boycott of Japanese goods enacted in 1932, the newly-empowered Japanese war machine sent four divisions of troops to Shanghai, gaining control of the port and surrounding areas.The Japanese openly exploited the puppet government of Manchuria and encouraged the highly-profitable opium trade. Finally, the Chinese decided to fight Japan, instead of accepting the generous offerings of settlement from the Japanese government. Many Japanese citizens preferred to seek peace and opposed the war with China, due to increasing economic hardships. Additionally, Japan's Army General Staff preferred to focus their military might on the Soviet Union. However, the Japanese army was not easily controlled. Several incidences, including attacks on an American gunboat, the British ambassador, and the vicious rampaging, following the capture of Nan King, were proof of this great difficulty.

In 1941, Japanese forces entered French Indochina (Cambodia, Laos, and Vietnam). The United States unsuccessfully attempted to persuade Japan to withdraw from China and southeast Asia through diplomatic channels. Finally, after a decade of claiming neutrality and observing a continuing military threat and expansion of Japanese and German forces, the United States of America declared war on Japan when our Pacific fleet was virtually destroyed by a questionable, *surprise* attack, while anchored at Pearl Harbor, Hawaii, on that infamous date of December 7, 1941.

Because of Japan's alliance with Germany, the United States soon joined the Allied war effort against both countries. Additionally, German forces continued to expand their occupation into most of Europe during 1941, as well. Soon, Hitler disregarded his nonaggression pact with Soviet leader Josef Stalin and invaded the Soviet Union, proving to be the first step down the path of destruction and collapse of his Third Reich.

In 1945, Germany and finally Japan, were defeated by the Allied Forces, at an irreplaceable expense of property and human lives. Furthermore, an *ushering in* of the Atomic Age, which instantly, killed hundreds of thousands of Japanese, forever altered the world's political and military policies. World War II resulted in the death of over 50 million people, including some 11 million, who perished in the Nazi death camps.

In 1978, according to his autobiography, *Just As I Am*, the Reverend Billy Graham when visiting the Auschwitz death camp, after laying a wreath at the Wall of Death and offering prayer, stated:

> *Auschwitz... stands as a warning for all humanity... that man is still capable of repeating and even multiplying the barbarism of Auschwitz. I... call upon Christians everywhere to work and pray for peace... The issues we face are not only political; they are also moral.*

Again, history recorded the demise of a centralized government imposing control upon its citizens by military means. Likewise, their nation's downfall could be attributed to the greed and corruption of power-hungry leaders exploiting their citizens, exercising Godlike judgments and privileges, and neglecting the wisdom of the teachings of the Lord's Word, through the ancient prophets and the new Covenant of Jesus the Christ.

Additionally, we mention political events, both *preceding* and *during* this recent attempt by a dictatorial government to conquer the world, to illustrate how dramatically, political decisions may affect your life. Typically, nations do not declare war without first experiencing a crescendo of political events, economic factors, and other forms of provocation, building up to a *breaking point*. The immense toll of human lives and societal sufferings forbids unilateral military decisions. Consequently, both justification and alternative solutions are sought by political debate.

These debates demand attentive and informed citizens to contribute their input. Unfortunately, there are not obvious signals indicating when *current* political issues will create an environment that will instigate a *future* war. Otherwise, most wars would certainly be avoided.

The Soviet Empire

After World War II, the Soviet Union, under the dictatorship of Josef Stalin, organized East Germany, Poland, Bulgaria, Czechoslovakia, Hungary and Romania into a group of satellite nations with Soviet-controlled Communist governments. The Communist's centralized government in Moscow exerted excessive societal controls throughout this region. The Soviet Union also exercised great influence in Yugoslavia and Albania during this same time period.

As the world knows, the Cold War with Russia ended during the Ronald Reagan administration. The greatly diminished Soviet Empire, and the once-satellite Communist nations are converting their governments to democracies and opening their economies to the principles of free trade, allowing their citizens the pleasures of liberty enjoyed by the western, industrialized world.

There is little need to restate the recent events throughout the Balkans, East Germany, and the Soviet Union, that have once again, proven that a centralized government that attempts to militarily enforce its administration of a nation by repressing individual rights, manipulating and owning private sectors of the economy, and prohibiting free enterprise, is destined for ruin. Time and time again, history has proven this to be true. This fact should create a very real appreciation for the freedoms enjoyed in the United States of America.

Have We Learned Anything?

Historical evidence proves there were legal documents empowering the dictators of these oppressive regimes. They did not break the laws of their nation; they merely changed or manipulated interpretation of existing laws, allowing their agendas to become sanctioned by their government's unique monopoly on enforcing its citizens behavior to follow the dictates of a radical minority's intimidating and unjust laws.

Do you think the German citizens could foresee the atrocities their nation would eventually commit when their currency was drastically devalued and they chose to forgo payments on their war debt? Of course not. However, that was one of the major political elements that allowed Adolph Hitler's empowerment. Popular public opinion supported their nation's default of World War I reparations.

When American sentiment swayed our Congress to enact trade-protectionist laws on agricultural imports, causing the debt-laden European countries that owed American and German banks to default, leading to major bank failures, the collapse of the New York Stock Exchange, and the ensuing Great Depression, do you think our Congress, or the American people foresaw the consequences of their actions?

Our nation's citizens must understand that there are not warning signs that flash every time a liberal agenda is successfully passed in our Congress and Senate. We will not see previews of a possible post-Americana life-style, reminding us of the consequences of our lack of patriotic interest and action, on the television or in the newspapers. Terrorists, rogue nations, and other external threats are more readily identifiable, and more easily fought by our nation's military and law-enforcement agencies. However, the American citizens are unprotected from an invisible enemy, the threat of our democracy and free enterprise system collapsing from the increasing weight of government interference in our personal and economic lives.

There are no mandates by either major political party that demand a strict adherence to the conservative policies of our Constitution. Political campaign contributors are the impetus for *both* major political party's agenda. Our national interests demand constant vigilance and monitoring. Encourage your representatives to pursue America's best interests, in lieu of, special-interest groups and their own reelection possibilities.

It is incredibly ironic that if our nation's leaders would selflessly pursue our nation's conservative interests and reduce special-interest group's influence in our nation's political arena, the American people would overwhelmingly support them for continued representation. Yet, few have the insight or political will to pursue this noble cause.

Hindsight is always so clear. However, there may be political decisions made today, which produce disastrous results for our nation in unforeseen circumstances in the future. That is why it is essential for *every* American to voice their opinion in the ballot boxes and to participate in the entire political process. It is commonly agreed that the wisdom of many is greater than the knowledge of a select few. Each of us *must* contribute our unique perspective and through that contribution, foster a larger, more balanced discussion of the issues our nation faces.

As a result of our efforts, the United States of America might avoid future calamities and possible ruin. If Americans from every neighborhood, background, ethnic origin and income level would contribute to a greater awareness of the implications of each political decision made on our behalf and follow through with action at the polls, we will have commenced our struggle to regain our nation's rightful destiny.

Chapter 5
Self-Indulgence Is Out!

Through trial and great error, we have learned that our own search for earthly pleasures is a meaningless quest. Likewise, our society must release its obsession with materialism. Individually, we must choose to seek wisdom and righteousness or continue our foolish pursuit of elusive, perishing pleasures. Throughout history, the rich and the poor share the same fate. We have a choice in the legacy we leave.

We the People must take into great consideration our every thought and deed, so as not to allow the irrational thoughts of an immoral society to plunge us into such foolish behavior. Our founding fathers were men of deep faith in the living God. As a result, we have been blessed with a legacy of freedom and liberty. Furthermore, we have been granted the privilege to pursue happiness; however, if we commit everything within our means to the seeking of pleasure and material objects, we lose the necessary balance in each of our lives that is required to continue our society's existence.

It appears that somehow we have allowed our priorities to be twisted and turned upside down. So called, *Modernism*, lacks a clear and concise expression of a strong political belief in the wisdom of the Constitution and the necessity for our belief in God. It denies the concept of individual accountability to protect our individual rights, economic prosperity and the future of this great nation. Consequently, we must continue our search in order to make sense amidst the confusion. You may hate politics, but it is our duty as Americans, to work with all diligence to restore Godly principles in our homes, communities, and in our nation's political arena.

Another aspect of the negative impact of materialism upon our society, is the deterioration of the family unit. In pursuit of our consumer-driven life-style, typically, both parents are required to work. This has resulted in many of our nation's children being deprived of their parents' loving devotion and instruction. For those fortunate enough to afford daycare services or receive government assistance, minimal wage child care providers strive to substitute parental supervision and care, typically, without proper resources and staffing. Furthermore, many children are simply left alone, without any supervision.

Granted, Americans are incredibly busy in their daily lives. However, is it possible that the distractions of materialism have influenced our priorities in a negative way? Should both parents work full-time to make the mortgage payments on the most expensive home we can afford, buy the most luxurious car, purchase designer clothes, continue to buy more and more until our closets, garages, and landfills are overflowing? Possibly, we could become more involved in our local church, school, or community functions, educating ourselves on the political issues of the day, and in our individual, *unique* way, make a difference.

During the most recent decade, we have ample evidence of corrupt leadership in our nation's highest and most revered office. Human nature is sinful, and everyone makes mistakes; however, we must continually strive to improve our lives by changing our behavior. We are hopeful that our recently-elected president, George W. Bush, will restore these values to that office.

Our nation's freedom is not an eternally-flowing spring, but requires vigil stewardship. We must appreciate and nurture this freedom, or risk losing it. We must stop ignoring the needs of our country. If we are not personally involved, we will be negatively affected in some manner. After all, are *We the People* not the government and the nation?

The average citizen is unaware of the implications and possible far-reaching consequences of the majority of most laws that are passed by our legislators. With the passage of many, amid the absence of our individual input, *our*

61

best interests are not fully considered. Americans have a plethora of information on our nation's history, literally, at their fingertips. For the first time in history, we have broad access to information, via the Internet, computer programs, books and documentary films. Americans must self-educate themselves on the essential issues and unwavering moral principles our founding fathers were willing to fight and die to preserve. There is no better time to commence your quest for knowledge.

What is the future of our great nation? What are we going to do to improve its chances of survival? These are the questions we should be asking ourselves. As the current benefactors of freedom, it is critical we pay attention to the affairs of our local, state and national governments. It should come as no surprise that some politicians forsake the majority and national interests, due to being swayed by special-interest groups. When this happens, the integrity of our political process is sorely compromised.

Since the beginning of modern civilization, history has recorded the downfall of nations that perished when their citizens failed to follow the eternal wisdoms found in the natural laws of liberty, truth and justice. Our nation's founders believed God intended mankind to live without physical or economic enslavement. However, as a result of extraneous government-legislated interference, our nation's future generations are enslaved by our legacy of monumental debt.

It is time for our nation to stop and contemplate the consequences which follow when Godly principles are set aside and new ones are adopted. It is time for each of us to pray to the Lord for guidance, giving Him glory for the wonderful gift of freedom, and the strength to stand up for its future. What sadness and what disastrous results will befall us, if we continue upon the irresponsible path we have allowed our nation to wander!

We must devote our efforts to seek out and elect honest, sincere, family-oriented Americans to leadership positions. Individuals with great integrity should be chosen. We need politicians who will represent society's best interests, instead of the self-serving individuals pursuing personal gain, or the misguided liberal reformer attempting to right all wrongs by continually enacting more federal laws. America needs each and every citizen to accept the challenge and become involved in their own self-governing.

Sadly, even our nation's courtrooms have allowed corruption to influence justice, as well. Sometimes it is no longer about truth and justice, but money and power. Who has the most political influence or power, or who is willing to spend the most money to purchase justice? America's judicial system must not allow justice and the enforcement of our nation's Constitution to be determined by external political and monetary influences. Greed, hatred, and corruption must be eliminated from our law enforcement agencies, courtrooms and political offices.

In order for this behavior to change, we *must* get involved. We must take note of the oppression that *exists* around us. Are you actively involved in a church, civic, or other group to prevent oppression, be a watchdog for justice, or to support your local law enforcement agencies in your area? If there isn't a local group, perhaps you could start one. If there is and you're not involved, join and maybe ask a friend to accompany you. Odds are, you will make new friends with similar concerns and interests.

Chapter 6

Government's Role

In most ways, our great nation, originally founded as a republic in 1776, has surpassed all other systems of government in the world. However, there is a common problem prevalent in our state and federal governments. A steady and continuous growth of government plagues our society. This growing financial burden upon our economy and nation is unsustainable. The principle reason big government continues as one of our greatest problems, has been best stated by German philosopher, F. Hoelderlin, who said:

The reason government is Hell is that we have tried to make it Heaven on earth.

We have attempted this *perfectionist theory* in America during the last century, trying one political experiment after another, with very dubious results.

Each year, Congress enacts many new laws in an attempt to patch loopholes in the existing laws, which were originally passed, in an effort to create equal results. In our efforts to create a better society, we have run the gamut searching for a system to cure all of our society's problems. We fail to see that we are expecting our government to produce something that it was never conceived or designed to accomplish. In order to improve mankind and society in general, we must consider the following two appropriate fundamentals.

First, government's primary function is the protection of each individual's liberties and personal property. Not to do so, ignores the basic precepts set forth by our founding fathers. It must be understood that government does not *provide* this liberty, it only *protects* the individual's God-given *right* to liberty.

Secondly, government must recognize that society is composed of individual citizens, which collectively, have the *same* protection and privileges as the individual. This means injustice must be prevented for society, as well as, the individual. No attempt by government to compromise the validity of this concept should *ever* be proposed.

Let's examine these two concepts. The first, simply states that government is the guarantor of each individual citizen's God-given rights and privileges for the pursuit of happiness and prosperity. Additionally, the government is responsible for enforcement of *just* laws and penalties for the damage or loss of personal property caused by others. Let us clarify, our government is not responsible for the *prevention* of the loss or damage, but for the *enforcement* of our society's laws punishing individuals committing these illegal actions. The primary and utmost responsibility of government is to protect our personal freedoms.

The second concept is much more complicated, less defined, and is the *controversial* challenge for our lawmakers. It leaves much room for interpretation. Many well-meaning politicians have eroded the primary concept by making decisions on our behalf that are intended to preserve the second concept. They pass unjust laws that affect society negatively, but by applying it equally to all Americans, justify their actions.

However, please understand... because the law is *applied* equally to all Americans, do not mistake this for *affecting* all Americans equally. These laws are written to grant special privileges for specific circumstances of a select minority. A simple illustration:

> *A supervised group of school children attending a county fair are given multi-colored, free-entry tickets. Addtionally, the supervisor, being aware that all the children of wealthy, influential parents with whom favor may be gained, possess red tickets, announces to the entire group that those children holding red tickets, in addition to free addmission, receive a free*

ride on the Ferris Wheel. All the children examine their tickets, some gleefully, but most are disappointed. This "appears" to justly administer special privileges to a few, since the rule was applied to the entire group. Obviously, "no one" is to blame that some children gained particular benefits and others did not. However, the lingering child that notices the commonality of the "lucky" group is reluctant to protest from fear of reprisals, due to the supervisor's unquestionable authority and obvious warning conveyed by a stern-jawed stare and firmly-gripped paddle.

Applied equally with intentional *unequal effects*. This is the basic principle behind the majority of our lawmakers' efforts. Their primary allegiance is to themselves, in the manifestation of the major contributors to their last election campaign or potential contributors to future campaigns.

This misguided effort advances the premise that individual citizens must voluntarily fit themselves, or else be forcefully compelled, to adjust to the equally-applied unjust laws of contemporary society. Thus, the *individual's* freedom of choice and action are severely limited or removed for the benefit of *society*. This simply means that our elected government officials decree what is right or wrong. Legality then, replaces Divine morality, as the prime measure of acceptable behavior on the part of the individual citizen.

When conformance to man-made rules of conduct is the basis for social acceptability, there is little incentive for individual achievement in any realm of human behavior beyond the officially, prescribed average or *norm*. Once a government attempts to rectify the mores of society by force of law, the economic system will suffer the same devastating consequences; for the society at large, must carry the burden for increased costs of law enforcement, lawmaking, and the essential supporting functions of government. Meanwhile individual productivity tends to decrease for the same reason that standards of personal behavior tend to stagnate or deteriorate... because there is no real incentive for anyone to exceed the *legal standard* of productivity or workmanship.

Obviously, there are limitations on each of our freedoms that begin when our individual freedom infringes upon those of our fellow citizens. However, beyond the necessary laws for public safety, many laws, including national defense, and foreign policy, are passed for the benefit of special-interest groups, hindering equal opportunities with attempts to either equalize results or grant unilateral benefits to a specific few.

Those who believe God is the Creator of the universe and all living creatures, and that human life on earth is only a proving ground for the eternal life of our immortal spirit, understand that each individual is responsible for the well-being of themselves and their family. The Lord intended for each of us to prosper according to our own abilities, efforts, and faith, and never promised that each of us would have equal lives on this earth, but that we are all equally, given the opportunity. Naturally, the elderly, invalid, widows and orphans are in need of government-administered assistance. But this assistance should be administered at the local level, the lowest level of government possible, to more efficiently and equitably, award assistance, instead of at the national level.

In reading God's Holy Word, we find Christ did not charge society with the responsibility for individual prosperity. However, He *did* teach individual responsibility. He allows us choices and He taught by examples of voluntary acts of kindness and love. He did not make demands on the Roman government for social improvements. He called upon individuals to improve themselves, which in turn, improves both society *and* government.

These points are intended to remind us that God gave us guidance, yet we continue to pass laws that broaden the intended purpose of government. Must our nation continually try to rewrite God's law? God is our only hope. We have seen ample evidence, since the beginning of time. We must realize the folly of departing from God's principles.

We the People have long since tired of meaningless contradictions by our political leaders. It is time to return to God's Word and follow His wisdom. We must not be complacent any longer. Americans must *awaken* and energize a grassroots effort to regain control of this country and their lives. Without each American's participation, the few will still control and manipulate our government's resources, at the expense of the many. It is your decision.

It is imperative that Americans understand our democratic system of government has not let us down. It is we, whom have let our democratic system of government down, by our lack of individual participation. The *good news* is that our participation is *all* that is required to once more set our nation upon the continued path to greatness.

We The People

Most of us are familiar with the brief Preamble of our nation's Constitution. It begins with *"We the People, of the United States of America"*.

We the People! What an inspirational concept! *We the People*, describes a nation granting all citizens an equal voice, not just the wealthy, or select few. Such a form of government was unique when our nation was founded in the 18th century. In reference to self-governing, history consists of mostly cruel and unjust stories of kings, queens, dictators and other self-appointed rulers proclaiming Divine birthright or inspiration. The idea of *We the People* challenged this tyranny of the past. It states that an informed citizenry is capable of self-rule by overseeing government's administration of their own affairs. Our Constitution aptly and comprehensively explains this process through majority rule, benefiting the majority, without sacrificing the individual's rights and freedoms.

Unfortunately, this great principle has been weakened and abused in recent years by our own indifference, our own lack of vigilance as the caretakers and shareholders of our great nation's freedom. It is not by action, but by our own inaction, that this great miracle of humanitarian self-rule is slipping from our grasp.

How frequently do we hear people say, *"I don't vote because my vote doesn't really matter"*? Now voting in itself is no great virtuous act of patriotism, but *intelligent* voting is *vital* to the proper function of our government. Each of us are uniquely composed of our own experiences, religious beliefs, moral values, and self-interest, both economically and personally. It is this unplanned dynamic of our society that creates a balanced, mutually-beneficial compromise in our government's decision-making. When this dynamic suffers from input, consequently, our government's decisions, or more specifically, its laws, are biased toward those whom have made the effort to establish their input.

Recently in a discussion with a person that admitted to never having voted in their entire life, the question, *"What could possibly be more important than the politics of your country?"* was posed. Their response was, *"Their religion"*. This reply was an honest one, a good one. Their religion meant more to them than the business of their nation's government.

Indeed, our personal religious beliefs are directly, more important than the affairs of our nation. God demands our ultimate allegiance, above all other matters, including those of our country. Yet, can we practice our religious beliefs without political freedom?

In 1776, Reverend John Witherspoon was the only clergyman to sign the Declaration of Independence. Reverend Witherspoon, understanding the importance of political liberty made his case:

> *There is not a single instance in history in which civil liberty was lost and religious liberty entirely preserved. If therefore we yield our temporal property, we at the same time deliver our conscience into bondage.*

Pastor Witherspoon's message crystallizes the significance of political freedom in preserving religious liberty.

Besides religion, some feel family is more important than the matters of government. Admirably, some place their personal responsibility to devoting time and caring for their loved ones above politics. However, a stable family life requires political freedom. Consider the population control of some socialized countries where an individual's ability or choice to have children is not the *ultimate* authority.

69

So therefore, if political freedom is essential to maintaining the freedoms that Americans hold dear, and the free enterprise system is essential to preserving our political freedom, must one ask the necessity of participating in our nation's politics to protect the free enterprise system from liberal attacks? It is not only our birthright, but the patriotic responsibility of every American citizen to defend this spontaneous miracle of economic self-expression.

The importance of our own personal opinion, our vote, in the electoral process must be clearly seen. Our entire country's freedom depends upon alert, informed citizens making certain that *We the People* are in command of our government.

National Defense

As our founding fathers intended, there are justifiable purposes for a strong, national government. The primary purpose of our government is the defense of our nation, our people, and our free society from any imposing forces, whether it be, individual, individually-organized, or a foreign government threat. This venerable cause, as Leonardo da Vinci surmised:

... to preserve the chief gift of nature, which is liberty.

should remain our nation's top priority and independent of political posturing in our nation's political debates. Naturally, poor fiscal management of our nation's military acquisitions should remain under scrutiny.

As an admirable example of the morally-correct use of America's military and economic strength, according to *An American Life, Ronald Reagan*, President Reagan wrote a letter to the Soviet president Leonid Brezhnev, contrasting the United States with historical world powers:

When WWII ended, the United States had the only undamaged industrial power in the world. Our military might was at its peak - and we alone had the ultimate weapon; the nuclear weapon, with the un-

*questioned ability to deliver it anywhere in the world.
If we had sought world domination then, who could
have opposed us? But the United States followed a
different course, one unique in all history of mankind. We used our power and wealth to rebuild the
war-ravaged economies of the world, including those
nations who had been our enemies.*

Every American citizen should demand our government provide a modern, capable military. We must never
become lax in our thoughts to consider the mounting threats
to our freedom. Likewise, we must demand an accountability of our government to spend *our* tax dollars as we would
spend them ourselves. It should no longer be acceptable or
tolerated, for our government to mismanage billions of taxpayer dollars in defense contracts. To allow our government
to continue this corrupt practice by not demanding accountability at the polls, is reprehensible, unpatriotic, and a self-
infliction of inevitable economic hardship.

It is an axiom of history that world powers with internal economic strife, collapse from the weight of their military. We must be heedful to history's lessons regarding efforts to militarily enforce our nation's interests, in lieu of,
continuing to create and expand economic *free*-trade partners that protect mutual interests.

Terrorism

The recent terrorist attacks on our nation are examples
of the perceived threat our democratic society imposes upon
the world's enemies of freedom. Why attack America? Perhaps our foreign policy and tactics *are* less than optimum,
allowing oppressive regimes to crystallize their citizens' frus-
trations against an easily, enviable enemy. However, these
typically, self-appointed leaders are motivated to attack
America because our country is the world's leader and front-
runner in the great societal experiment of individual freedoms and liberty. When properly exercised, our freedoms
prevent the rise to power of dictators, who rule with oppressive laws, enslaving their citizens to a life of poverty and

71

hardship, while they and their supporters, enjoy the benefit of their nation's productivity.

However, there has been a recent surge of increasing regulation designed to protect the average American. A new cabinet-level agency named Homeland Defense, yet without the same accountability to Congress, is charged with implementing additional protective measures against terrorism. Although we agree some areas of security in Americans' daily lives have been ignored and need attention, there must be a continued vigilance to prevent our privacy, our freedoms, and our way of life, from being stolen from us, under the guise of protection.

Pre-WWII Germany imposed protections on their citizens to protect them from evil, as well. The German government treated Jewish citizens as evil sub-humans, while German propaganda proclaimed the political correctness of their genocidal actions and eventually, the German government outlawed any citizen's efforts of assistance. Social control is *not* the responsibility of any government, but *protecting* the individual's *liberties*, is the responsibility of *every* government.

Certainly, it is our federal government's responsibility to protect us from our nation's enemies and with an ever-changing, global political scene, there are special needs that must be addressed. However, citizens must maintain a watchful eye to prevent zealous politicians and bureaucrats from overstepping their authority. Wiretapping, profiling, and personal property searches, are all areas of possible abuse. Quoting the 19th century French journalist, Frederic Bastiat:

> *If a right does not exist for any one of the individu als whom collectively we designate... as a nation, how can it exist for that fraction of the nation having merely delegated rights, which is the government?*

Usama Bin Laden understands the true nature of our nation's resources and desires to strike fear in the heart of each American. He hopes this will create a liberal overreaction to his efforts, which will stymie the American spirit. Bin Laden, an advocate of oppression, desires our leaders to implement martial law, or other totalitarian forms of societal control. Under our country's form of government, the American people, their diversity, ingenuity, and liberty, are the foundation for which the entire world's future and prosperity are built. If fear is allowed to creep into the lives of Americans, immobilizing our economy, destabilizing our global political influences, and worse, creating an environment that breeds further erosion of our freedoms to the point of finally choking off our enjoyment of life, liberty, and freedom, each individual's personal motivation for living life to the fullest, will have been eliminated.

This is the motivation that creates terrorist action. If America does not allow them to succeed, and stands vigilant for the continued protection of our civil liberties, eventually their actions will become meaningless, thus eliminating them from relevance. The entire world is watching our nation, as we struggle to deal with the consequences of the terrorists' attacks, pursue justice, and implement security measures to deter future attacks.

As Americans, we have rallied together to heal our friends, family, and fellow citizens dealing with the emotional aspects of the September 11 attacks. We have contributed generously of our time, money and prayers. As Americans, we have also supported President Bush's leadership of the *War on Terrorism,* as he seeks justice for the victims and their families.

As Americans, we must also take action as the conservators of our liberties, by refusing to allow our way of life to be eliminated. Do not let the fear of future attacks overwhelm your senses. The margin between our founding father's original concept of freedom in this country, and the confines of socialism has been narrowed dramatically in the last century. Americans must resist knee-jerk reactions that cripple the soul of our nation.

Clearly, there are changes required in our public transportation industry, but Americans must resist the fear mongers' overreaction. Removing an individual's fingernail clippers from carry-on luggage by completely searching their possessions, reeks of pre-WWII Germany. In another recent incident, a congressman of Arabic descent, even after submitting his congressional ID and an accompanying fellow congressman vouching on his behalf, *and* after a thorough search, was still refused admission on a flight because of the *computer* system's profiling. As a final result, he was told he could fly the following day.

We are concerned that under the present circumstances, the erosion of our liberties may not be evident. However, consider a possible scenario immediately after simultaneous, widespread terrorist attacks. Our nation's leaders would be forced to seriously consider the implementation of stricter social controls, with the very *real* legal possibility of Martial Law, as defined under United States Senate Report 93-549, which we review shortly.

Economically, if market forces are unhindered, our free enterprise system will eventually ease many problems. For example, if the delays, inconveniences, and intrusions of privacy become a greater perceived negative than the positive benefits of air travel, the market will react. The airlines will be forced to hire additional counter personnel, implement less intrusive, but equally as thorough inspections, even design structural changes, or lose market share to alternative means of public and private transportation.

If one does not exist that is acceptable to the public, one will be created, and/or modified to fulfill the market demands. The dynamics of a free society at work, without government intervention, exhibit the fluidity of nature. An economic void cannot exist for an extended period of time without human innovation occupying its space.

However, if special-interest groups successfully lobby Congress to maintain or gain unfair market advantages, these corrections may not occur, or *worse,* conditions may deteriorate. This in turn, wastes resources and productivity, which can never be regained. This phenomena is the source of many burdens upon our economy, lowering our productivity, standard of living, and wasting humanity's most precious commodity: our *time* on this earth.

Where is the line? It is not for us to say, but as a nation we must resolve these issues with discernment and rationality, instead of fear and oppression.

The Threat Of Government

Our nation's founding fathers had a solid understanding of why *We the People* should be in control of their government's politics. Even before the Declaration of Independence and the adoption of our Constitution, Americans grasped the value of liberty; thus, giving rise to the eternal precepts for the self-governing of our nation.

Alexander Hamilton, clearly stated his understanding of America's God-given freedoms:

> *The only freedom worth achieving is a freedom which puts each of us at something he can do and sets before him, as a personal and individual responsibility, the management of his activities, relations, and possessions so that in the end he owes not any man.*

The Connecticut blacksmith or the Virginian farmer might have been unable to read, but they understood Hamilton's meaning. Likewise, they also appreciated Thomas Jefferson's simple, but profound definition of government which properly respects individual freedom. Jefferson stated:

> *The true foundation of republican government is the equal right of every citizen, in his person and property, and in their management.*

Unfortunately, this rings with a clarity of vision seldom understood by modern politicians.

Insightful leaders like Hamilton and Jefferson understood that government was necessary for freedom to exist. It was evident to them that individuals had the God-given right to *life, liberty, and the pursuit of happiness*, and that government was *not* the provider or creator of those rights, but the protector. However, government tends to encroach upon these freedoms of the individual and *We the People* must be ever vigil to defend against the loss of our rightful heritage.

The Declaration of Independence directly challenged the infringements of individual liberty by the monarchal government of King George III. The Declaration proclaims:

He has erected a multitude of New Offices, and sent hither swarms of Officers to harass our people, and eat out their substance. He has combined with others to subject us to a jurisdiction foreign to our constitution, and unacknowledged by our laws.

Later, while considering the Constitution of the United States, James Madison wisely wrote:

If men were angels, no government would be necessary. If angels were to govern men, neither external nor internal controls on government would be necessary. In framing a government which is to be administered by men over men, the great difficulty lies in this, you must first enable the government to control the governed, and in the next place oblige it to control itself.

Madison had a healthy distrust of government, because he understood the inherent nature of government and mankind. Any constitution or government would be imperfect. Imperfect, due to the fact that both would be the work of imperfect human beings. A *just* government required a *limited* amount of power and authority to effectively protect individual life, liberty and private property. That authority, however, could easily be abused and corrupted. Government could become a deadly destroyer, instead of the great protector of liberty.

Thus, the Constitution specifically defines and limits the powers of government. On the other hand, the first ten Amendments to the Constitution define individual rights, including freedom of assembly, speech, and religion. In a firm balance, we have the limited powers of government on one side and the *inalienable* rights of individuals on the other.

The preservation of personal freedom stands out as

the primary function of government. To accomplish this, government must both assure national defense, as well as, enforce society's laws protecting law-abiding citizens against domestic criminals. Jefferson summed up the role of legitimate government:

A wise and frugal government, which shall restrain men from injuring one another, shall leave them otherwise free to regulate their own pursuits and shall not take from their mouth of labor the bread it has earned. This is the sum of good government.

Excessive government interference into the social and economic affairs of a free society, attempting to alter the natural and eternal laws of God, is a mortal's folly. We must not allow atheistic attempts to legislate morality and legality conflict with the Divine wisdom of natural law. Dr. Martin Luther King Jr., argued this point by recalling:

We can never forget that everything Hitler did in Germany was legal and everything the Hungarian freedom fighters did in Hungary was illegal.

Government's Legal Right To Dictatorship

On March 9, 1933, President Roosevelt declared the United States in a State of Emergency, and our government bankrupt with Executive Orders 6073, 6102, 6111, and 6260. Roosevelt's Executive Orders, in concert with, *The Trading with the Enemy Act*, Public Law 65-91, passed by the 65th Congress on October 6, 1917, supplanted the United States Constitution with a military rule of the Commander-in-Chief, the President of the United States of America.

President Roosevelt declared the American citizens an enemy of the government, thus allowing our government to subject us to its desires, instead of a government *By the people* and *For the people*. In the original *Trading with the Enemy Act of 1917* passed on Oct. 6, 1917, under the *Trading with the Enemy Act*, Section 2, subdivision (c), Chapter 106 - Enemy is defined as *"other than citizens of the United*

States..." On March 9, 1933, Chapter 106, Section 5, subdivision (b) of the Trading with the Enemy Act of Oct.6 1917 (40 Stat. L. 411) amended as follows "...any person within the United States.." See H.R. 1491.

Our own government is considered a belligerent nation under international law of nations. Such is their control of the American people, that our government can repossess private property, unless each licensee (citizen) pays tribute (taxes) to purchase protection from it.

According to the previously-mentioned, 93rd Congressional Senate Report No. 93-549, 1st Session, November 19, 1973, on the relevance of the State of Emergency declared by President Roosevelt:

> *A majority of people of the United States have lived all of their lives under emergency rule. For 40 years, freedoms and governmental procedures guaranteed by the Constitution have in varying degrees been abridged by laws brought into force by states of national emergency...*

Under the declared State of Emergency:

> *The President may: Seize property, organize commodities, assign military forces abroad, institute Martial Law, seize and control transportation and communication, regulate operation of private enterprise, restrict travel, and in a plethora of particular ways, control the lives of all American citizens. — Senate Report 93-549; Senate Resolution 9, 93d Congress, 1st. Session (III) 1973*
> *See: Chapter 1, Title 1, Section 48, Statute 1, March 9, 1933; Proclamation 2038; Title 12 U.S.C 95b*

On June 3, 1994, President Clinton issued Executive Order 12919, which specified the federal agencies' mechanisms for exerting controls, and defined their resources available, on a permanently, perpetual basis.

We are NOT a free people, sovereign over our lives.

We do not live in a republic, as originally declared in 1776. We now live in a democracy, which by definition, does not enforce the inalienable rights of mankind, but the wishes of the majority, or those that *control* and *influence* the delegated authority of the majority.

This is why it is *imperative* that Americans exert their control over government by participating in our political processes and elections. Just as Adolph Hitler *legally* seized absolute power in pre-WW II Germany, the legal mechanisms *exist* in our government that would permit a legal seizure of authoritarian rule in our own country. It is more critical than *ever*, that we elect moral representatives to administer our governing. Otherwise, we must accept the consequences of our inattentiveness, however distasteful and burdensome they may be, or face violent conflict.

Chapter 7
Social Reformers

One source of opposition to our free enterprise system is found in communism. When Karl Marx, the father of communism died, only eight people attended his funeral. The ideas which he expounded should have been given the same insignificant burial. Marx theorized that with the coming industrial revolution, the capitalists would exploit the worker and corner the wealth. To rectify this supposed situation, he suggested that the tools of production be seized for the public good. Owners' objections would be met with force! Thus, stealing at gunpoint was justification in his atheistic ideology. It is interesting to note that in societies where Marxist ideas have been employed, the Utopian society has failed to materialize. Quite the contrary, the controlled economy has only succeeded in sharing the poverty.

While Russia was boasting that she would outstrip the American economy, Japan, a free enterprise nation, booted Russia from the number two slot on the scale of world economies. Marx's new philosophy turned out to be nothing more than socialism with new terminology, appealing to that spark of larceny that lurks in every human heart. The communist concept gave impetus to power politics, while affording sanctuary to corrupt politicians.

Communists disdain any free order, for the essence of a communistic society is total control. The Iron Curtain, propaganda, government ownership or control of industry, and personal consumption dictates, are all instruments of societal control.

We must be reminded that Marx did not call his economic system outlined in the Manifesto, a communist system, he called it socialism. That is precisely what it is, not only according to the self-admitted Marx, but also according to any reliable, political science text or encyclopedia.

Lenin wrote in his classic work, *State and Revolution:*

> *... It has never entered the head of any socialist to promise that the highest phase of communism will 'actually' arrive... as long as the highest phase of communism has 'not' arrived, the socialists demand the strictest control, by society, and by the state, of the quantity of labor and the quantity of consumption.*

No matter how you define it, how it is introduced, or even by what name you call it, a government-*owned*, *planned*, or *controlled* economic system is the very antithesis of free enterprise. It is industrial monopoly of the very *highest* order, and as such, cannot be expected to be any less stagnating than any other type of illegal monopoly.

It is agreed that a limited amount of government regulation is necessary to prevent individual malpractices in a free enterprise system. However, the use of government regulations to control a nation's production inhibits the interplay of those economic forces which make the free enterprise system the best provider of mankind's material needs, and simultaneously, allowing the bodily and spiritual freedom essential for the *pursuit of happiness*.

Can't We All Just Get Along?

Still another source of opposition to the free enterprise system came with the advent of the Nuclear Age. Presently, an unusual philosophy has found favor which purports that one must get along at all costs, even if it means the compromise of basic moral beliefs. It dictates, among other things, that to avoid conflict, competition must be abandoned, or at least, subdued.

This philosophy infers that competition leads to a conflict among people, between industries, between nations, the *haves* and the *have-nots*. So, if competition is abolished, we then have an atheistic attitude in which there is no reward or punishment for sin, crime, effort or laziness. Therefore, natural law would be forsaken and differences between people, their productivity, their ability, worthiness, etc., would be eliminated. Consequently, our individual motivation to pursue happiness and prosperity would be greatly curtailed. In turn, our economic free enterprise system will suffer, resulting in less competition, and increased inefficiencies

Sociologists call this system *environmental* control of people. The proponents of this system hope to remove the causes of war by improving society and reducing conflicts among people. The conflicts which they see as causes of war are social, racial, religious, nationalistic, and of course, economic. Are there others?

This group of *social engineers* sponsor and promote pandering welfare laws, unjust equal opportunity laws, internationalism, disarmament, monopolistic unionism and other liberal programs to redistribute the wealth. It seems appropriate to point out, if these goals are accomplished, there would be little for which to hope, little for which to aspire, and precious little to inspire life.

Their approach to an avoidance of future human sufferings runs cross-current to the religious concept that humans are a free moral agent. When humans are prohibited from making a wrong decision, there really is no choice at all. Jesus the Christ, taught in order to change society, individuals must change their heart. These proponents of social engineering teach that to change society, you simply *pass laws* forcing man to conform to the new confines of government. Christ did not advocate changing society to improve mankind, but rather, each individual should improve themselves, which would, of course, improve society.

Much can be said for the lofty goals that these socialist-minded individuals desire to achieve. But the solutions which they offer strike at the very foundation of the principles upon which this nation was founded, and to date, continues to provide for its prosperity. Unfortunately, many citizens have unwittingly joined their ranks against free enterprise, attracted by these worthy goals for humanity. Worse yet, some economic reformers offering an unrealistic level of social and economic security, which would seriously harm our free enterprise system, have occupied influential positions in our government.

According to *The Congressional Record*, Sept. 26, 1961, Professor Arthur Schlesinger Jr., wrote:

> *... neither communism, with its despotism, nor capitalism with its instability, nor fascism with its combination of the two, provide attractive solutions to the problem of how to live in a modern industry and a modern state. Is there another possibility? Has noncommunist, libertarian socialism a future? Abstracting the question for a moment from current political activities, one must answer that there is no inherent reason why democratic socialism should not be possible...*

But, if a democracy grants individual freedoms, and socialism means government ownership or control of productive property, then the term democratic socialism is self-contradictory. It is a fundamental principle that personal ownership of property is basic to all freedoms.

History has proven this conflict with human nature is unstable. There can be no liberty without an individual measure or reward for productivity or innovation. The *individual* human spirit cannot be harnessed by the entire weight of *all* mankind. Humans must be left to their *own* devises to fulfill their dreams and to pursue their *own* happiness. Inversely, human nature will allow those that *choose* to live from the efforts of others, to do so, as well.

Professor Arthur Schlesinger Jr., is but one example of influential persons that have actively sought to replace the free enterprise system with a system of centralized government planning and control. However, Professor Schlesinger stands out as a particularly worrisome example, because he served as an advisor to President John F. Kennedy and remains highly influential in many intellectual circles.

Professor Schlesinger's paper reveals his conspiracy with fellow socialists, planning many years ago to wage their protracted war against our free enterprise system. Again, quoting from his writing:

> *... If socialism (i.e. The ownership by the state of all*

significant means of production) is to preserve de-
mocracy, it must be brought about step by step in
such a way which will not disrupt the fabric of
custom, law, and mutual confidence upon which
personal rights depend. That is, the transition must
be piecemeal; it must be parliamentary; it must
respect civil liberties and due process of law.

Here again, in self-contradictory fashion, Professor
Schlesinger speaks of respecting *civil liberties* and *personal
rights*, even as he seeks to impose an economic system which
denies the most basic right, the right to own and control
productive property, upon which all true human liberty must
be based.

More importantly perhaps, we should consider why
Dr. Schlesinger advises a gradual approach. He explains:

... The classical argument against this gradualism
was that the capitalist ruling class would resort to
violence rather than surrender its prerogatives.
Here, as elsewhere, the Marxists enormously
overestimated the political courage and will of the
capitalists. In fact, in the countries where capital-
ism really triumphs, it has yielded with far better
grace (that is, displayed more cowardice than the
Marxist scheme predicted). The British experience
is illuminating in this respect, and the American
experience is not uninstructive. There is no sign in
either nation that the capitalists are mounting
much opposition.

With respect for Dr. Schlesinger's well-meaning intentions as a tireless advocate of *affirmative government*,
this must be recognized as an attack against our free enterprise system and ensuing economic and personal freedom.

In the formative stages of our government, our forefathers relied heavily upon the Judeo-Christian concept of
God, an understanding that God is supreme and rules the
universe; created mankind in its image, made humanity sovereign and gave them the freedom of choice as an individual

to determine their own destiny. To ensure and perpetuate this God-given freedom, our forefathers established a government that was forbidden to trespass on these eternal individual birthrights.

Revolutionary in concept and expression, our government was the product of immense work. Much time was given to prayer, as a means to maintain the truth in ideology, as applied to the self-governing of a nation. Fortunately, the Colonies had previous self-governing experiences, such as Plymouth Colony, that reminded them of the errs and failure of a communal or socialist system.

Consequently, Plymouth Colony might possibly be attributed to being the first self-governing experiment with a free enterprise system in this country. After the demise of their communal effort and the implementation of a free enterprise system, Governor William Bradford recorded in his diary:

> *This had very good success, for it made all very industrious, so that much more corn was planted than otherwise would have been.*

However, this was not the first time socialism had been tried and failed, but it is a noteworthy case in which socialism failed, although instituted under the most favorable conditions. Nevertheless, socialism did not work *then*, it has *never* worked, and there is no recent cause to believe that it will *ever* work. It constrains and conflicts with the inherent nature of humanity.

Chapter 8

How Did We Get Here?

What is the future of the empire? In a 1943 address at Harvard University, Britain's Prime Minister Sir Winston Churchill predicted, *"The empires of the future are the empires of the mind."* Churchill was undoubtedly, referring to the competition of ideologies for people's minds, as was then occurring between the competing communist and democratic ideologies. But, his prediction could also apply to the situation at the beginning of the Third Millennium. Some observers think we may be witnessing the beginnings of a global cultural community in which people around the world are linked by telecommunications and the Internet. This global community is dedicated to the free exchange of information and ideas, certainly an *empire of minds*.

This emerging global society is also devoted to the pursuit of wealth, the nonstop electronic movement of money and consumerism. Much of the latter is based upon American popular culture, which like an expanding empire of old, appears to be spreading over the planet, a world given over to capitalist enterprise and the *good life*.

However, as the leader of this global movement, Americans must search their souls, objectively examine their familial situations, and discover within themselves a median life-style, which will lead our country, thus the world, on a sustainable and spiritually-fulfilled journey. We must remain cognizant of corporate America, through self-serving interests, leading the charge of consumerism and its powerful influence on our government's domestic and foreign policies. Only through each American's individual involvement and awareness, will our nation be able to temper our federal government's misguided efforts to perpetuate this popular binge of consumerism at taxpayer expense.

Legacies Of The Great Depression

Much of today's opposition to the free enterprise system dates back to the beginning of the great economic depression of 1929. The resulting economic hardships caused many Americans to become disenchanted with free enterprise. The widespread deprivation of the basic essentials needed for survival among millions of Americans created a deep resentment. These unfavorable conditions continued for a prolonged period. The lack of immediate and direct affirmative action by President Hoover to address the population's woes, created a federal intervention mandate for the future survival of any presidential candidate.

Our purpose in discussing this topic is to counter those liberals heralding the Great Depression as an example of the failure of the free enterprise system. As previously discussed, in addition to the many domestic factors that created this great economic tragedy, there were little-mentioned external factors that significantly contributed to the collapse of the New York Stock Exchange, major bank failures, and consequently, our economy falling into an extended depression era.

To review, the *Panic of 1837* was instigated by the Rothschild-controlled Bank of England as revenge against President Andrew Jackson for withdrawing all government deposits from the Second Bank of the United States, another Rothschild-controlled bank. President Jackson vehemently opposed a central-banking policy, including currency debt, *and* publicly-acknowledged debt. His 1832 reelection campaign slogan was *"JACKSON and NO BANK!"* He had previously fired 2,000 of the 11,000 federal employees, due to the influence of the bankers. This created a fierce battle between President Jackson and the international bankers seeking access to the American public debt. As an end result to the *Panic of 1837*, the Rothschilds purchased American securities for *one* cent on the dollar! They later used this capital to finance J.P. Morgan, whom aided their efforts to control and profit from American industrial advances.

Thus, it is reasonable to consider that politicians, foreign and domestic capitalists, and liberal social reformers may have nefariously affected our nation in 1929. Clearly, the Hoover administration's tightening of our nation's money supply during a time of widespread farm losses contributed to the failure of many rural banks. The bank failures, coupled with excessive personal debt, and a panicked America selling a record sixteen million shares in a crashing bear market on October 29, 1929, forced our economy into the Great Depression. During the thirteen years following this catastrophe, approximately nine thousand banks failed, wiping out millions of Americans' savings.

President Herbert Hoover, believing in a laissez-faire government, vetoed several bills aimed at relieving the effects of the ensuing economic depression. Confident that our nation's business community and the free enterprise system could overcome the collapse of our economy, he resisted increasing our federal government's power.

Although, we're inclined to agree with his basic conservative assumptions, President Hoover was not accurately gauging the depth of the problem. The state and local governments weakened by a tightening of currency, rapidly depreciating land values and major unemployment, simply did not have the resources, or the ability to borrow them, to adequately provide food, clothing and shelter for the nation's newly-impoverished citizens.

The Great Depression did not occur independent of federal and foreign interference, and required federal interdiction to ease the resulting hardships, as well. Finally, President Hoover grasped the enormity and self-feeding nature of the Great Depression, and created the Reconstruction Finance Corporation (RFC) agency, which loaned capital to cash-starved railroads, banks, and other major institutions that were vital to the nation's recovery.

However, when Franklin D. Roosevelt assumed office in 1933, responding to a mandate for federal intervention, his administration immediately introduced sweeping legislation, creating banking and labor regulatory agencies, such as, the Securities and Exchange Commission (SEC), the Federal Deposit Insurance Corporation (FDIC), and the National Labor Relations Board (NLRB), in an effort to avoid a similar future crisis. As previously mentioned, President

Roosevelt also declared the United States federal government *bankrupt* and in a *State of Emergency* with Executive Orders 6073, 6102, 6111, and 6260. This granted Roosevelt broad latitude in governing our nation's affairs.

President Roosevelt's *New Deal* also included the Social Security Act, an easily-justifiable, more politically-acceptable, significant tax increase. Where else could such a tax increase be laid, except the feet of the elderly, invalid, and widowed? Interestingly, Congress has never acquired the constraint or courage to restrict its revenue to that specific purpose, creating enormous unfunded liabilities.

According to the Cato Project On Social Security Privatization, *Dismantling The Pyramid: The Why and How of Privatizing Social Security*, written by Professor Karl Borden, an economics professor at the University of Nebraska, published August 14, 1995:

> *Social Security is an unfunded pay-as-you-go system, fundamentally flawed and analogous in design to illegal pyramid schemes. Government accounting creates the illusion of a trust fund, but, in fact, excess receipts are spent immediately. The government's own actuaries predict the system will be bankrupt by 2030, but Social Security could face financial crisis as early as 2014.*
>
> *The liabilities already created, which are unrecognized by the government accounting system, represent sunk costs that cannot be recovered. Only adjustments in spending patterns can pay for those commitments. Short-term fixes to increase revenue or reduce benefits will be unsuccessful in the long run. ... Reform is long overdue. If we fail to act soon, our children will either inherit a bankrupt system or be forced to pay an impossibly high level of taxes.*

If interested in reviewing the entire study, contact the Cato Institute, 1000 Massachusetts Avenue NW, Washington, DC 20001, or access the information on their web-site:

www.cato.org/pubs/ssps/ssp1.html

Two initiatives by the Roosevelt administration, the creation of the National Recovery Administration (NRA) and the Agricultural Adjustment Administration (AAA) were ruled unconstitutional by the Supreme Court. In May 1935, in *Schechter Poultry Corp. vs. the United States*, the NRA was found unconstitutional on the basis that the compulsory-code, which empowered the Roosevelt administration to set hours of work, rates of pay, and the fixing of prices, was improperly delegating legislative powers to the executive; while major components of the AAA, which utilized coercive taxes, forcing cotton and tobacco farmers to limit the crops they sold, were ruled unconstitutional in 1936.

Many justify President Roosevelt's efforts as well-meaning, however the American citizens granted a precedence for relinquishing individual and economic rights to our federal government without demanding accountability. Furthermore, in addition to the cost of administration, the actual expense of our nation's recovery programs were financed, creating a trend of ever-increasing, government debt.

Perhaps one of the least recognized, but highly impacting legacies of the Great Depression, is the change in *attitude* of the American people. Due to the deprived life-style of many Americans during the Great Depression, materialism became a national mind-set. An entire generation became obsessed to acquire the comforts and life-styles, which many lost or never had during those difficult times.

Admirably, as their families grew, they strived to offer their children these same luxuries without demanding any effort or contribution on their part to attain them. This *something-for-nothing* attitude that many of the children of the fifties and sixties developed, combined with their parents' materialistic life-style, laid the foundation upon which the last few generations have built.

Unfortunately, these traits have impacted our society negatively. John Howard wrote in *Saturday Review*:

> *During this third of a century there have been few voices of intellectual or cultural prominence asserting and defending the interests of the entire society, in fact, that has been an era in which the parts have*

been granted virtually, unquestioned dominance over the whole. The large debates have been about which of the competing interest groups shall prevail, not whether the common welfare would be served or injured by the outcome of an issue. We here, in the United States produced several generations of cultural orphans... who have little knowledge and even less application of their heritage of freedom, or the struggles and sacrifices, which produced it. We have inadvertently engaged in a kind of unilateral intellectual disarmament, which could prove more devastating to the causes of liberty than would the voluntary destruction of our defense arsenals.

Furthermore, this *something for nothing* attitude has infiltrated every nook and cranny of our federal government's bureaucracy. We like to think our bureaucrats comprehend that the federal government is an *expense* to the nation and not an unlimited revenue source. However, according to their continued fiscally-irresponsible actions, we are forced to question this premise.

Perhaps the French journalist and constitutional political economist, Frederic Bastiat's observation in his essay, *The State*, best describes this phenomena:

The state is the great fictitious entity by which every one seeks to live at the expense of everyone else.

The National Debt

Although President Jackson lays claim to the only president that administered a totally, debt-free government, prior to President Roosevelt using the Great Depression to legitimize our government's new debt, the United States of America operated its government within a reasonably, balanced budget. George Washington, in his *Farewell Address to the People of the United States,* admonished the American citizens on a stable public credit:

...cherish public credit. One method of preserving it

*is to use it as sparingly as possible... avoiding like-
wise, the accumulation of debt... it is essential that
you... bear in mind, that towards the payment of debts
there must be Revenue, that to have Revenue there
must be taxes; that no taxes can be devised, which
are not... inconvenient and unpleasant...*

It must be mentioned that as the world's largest debtor, the United States of America (you and I) are becoming increasingly, dependent upon the nonelected, politically-appointed Federal Reserve Chairman for our economic well-being. Although Federal Reserve profits, above and beyond self-regulated expenses, are returned to the U.S. Treasury, there is the potential manipulation of the world's financial markets by international financiers.

Additionally, on the issue of government's right to issue currency without borrowing or subjecting our nation to the influences of foreign capitalists, Benjamin Franklin wrote in his autobiography:

*The colonies would gladly have borne the little tax
on tea and other matters, had it not been that
England took away from the colonies their money,
which created unemployment and dissatisfaction. The
inability of the colonists to get power to issue their
own money permanently out of the hands of George
III and the International Bankers was the Prime
reason for the Revolutionary War.*

The obvious conflict of currency debt is comparable to the concept of master-slave. The slave's interest in being *freed* is in direct conflict with the master's interest in *maintaining* the yoke of labor. The interesting aspect of this situation is that the above-described relationship was intended by our founding fathers to describe the citizens as the masters, and our government, as their slave. However, today one must question these roles.

The current low interest rates allow reduced federal payments on our national debt's interest, thus reducing our government's annual budget requirements. Therefore, unusually low interest rates conceal the true nature of the overwhelming debt left for our children to pay. Meanwhile, political pressures motivate our nation's leaders to continue spending borrowed money for their constituency, thus assuring reelection.

Likewise, the Federal Reserve Bank's board of directors and shareholders are interested in a continuing return by the most creditworthy customer in the world: the government of the American people. The Fed chairman tempers his private shareholders' demands for profits, by balancing public opinion, economic indicators, political pressures and the American surety, with private interests.

Our government monitors and manipulates the cost-of-living (COL) index through various industry-specific subsidies. In an effort to fight runaway spending by our federal government, our elected representatives require federal employees, retirees, and pensioners to limit their annual income raises in relationship to the COL index. Contrastively, aware of the deceitfulness of the propagandized COL, our elected officials regularly increase their own wages, much more liberally. As taxpayers, we certainly appreciate their thoughtfulness.

According to our federal General Accounting Office's (GAO) report, which was included in the 104th Congressional Committee on Government Reform and Oversight's report titled, *Federal Government Management: Examining Government Performance As We Near The Next Century,* on September 24, 1996:

> *$125 billion in Federal debt is delinquent. That is 37 percent of all debt owed. An additional $5 to $6 billion of criminal debt is outstanding. The amount of delinquent debt is climbing steadily.*

To clarify the report, the debt which is being discussed, is only the current debt payments, not the entire federal government's debt. Our government is bankrupt, but continues to spend beyond its means, without regard for the long-term consequences awaiting our children.

Presently, our federal government has borrowed on

our behalf, the staggering amount of *$30 trillion*, which is nearly $108,000 for *every* American man, woman, and child alive! The key to motivating Americans to stop this insanity, may be to help them understand that the government only borrows on our behalf. That is ***OUR*** debt, not the governments! Only America's small-businesses and corporations generate any productivity which creates wealth for its workers and owners. In turn, an increasing portion is *siphoned off* to pay for the governing of our lives.

As every American knows, if you are delinquent on your current debt, have no real solutions to offer, and in fact, are spending even *more* money than you can possibly repay, you are ***not*** a good candidate for additional loans from *anyone*! That is, unless you are the United States government, empowered by the good faith of the American people and manipulated by self-serving politicians.

The challenge of removing politics and reelection from our political leaders' concerns, is apparently, extremely difficult, if not impossible. Difficult business decisions are *not* being made in our nation's capital. Instead, we are leaving our inattentive and politically-powerless children beneath a mountain of debt.

In his autobiography, Benjamin Franklin warned:

The burden of debt is as destructive to freedom as subjugation by conquest.

On May 2, 1992, Texas Congressman, Henry B. Gonzalez, Chairman of the House of Representatives Committee on Banking, Finance and Urban Affairs, discussing *National And International Thievery In High Places,* states:

We are bankrupted. We are insolvent on every level of our national life, whether it is corporate, whether it is just plain you and I out there with the life of debt that we have all piled up, private debt, credit cards and what not, or whether it is the government. We are insolvent. How long will it take before that nasty mega-truth is conveyed?

According to *The Congressional Record,* January 19, 1976, page 240, Maryland Congresswoman Marjorie S. Holt addressing the Speaker of the House on the topic of international *authorities* (bankers) introducing a superior claim to American interests:

> *How do you like the idea of international authorities controlling our production and our monetary system, Mr. Speaker? How could any American dedicated to our national independence and freedom tolerate such an idea? America should never subject her fate to decisions by such an assembly, unless we long for national suicide. Instead, let us have independence and freedom... If we surrender our independence to a new world order... we will be betraying our historic ideals of freedom and self-government. Freedom and self-government are not outdated. The fathers of our Republic fought a revolution for those ideals, which are as valid today as they ever were. Let us not betray freedom by embracing slave masters; let us not betray self-government with world government; let us celebrate Jefferson and Madison, not Marx and Lenin.*

Yet, we have already done so. The Federal Reserve Act of 1913, required the United States government to pledge the assets of the American people as collateral. This was reconfirmed in 1933, when President Roosevelt declared our nation bankrupt, to include present and *future* assets. Our leaders have quietly, and unconstitutionally, pledged our financial future to international capitalists.

Congressman Henry B. Gonzalez continuing his *National And International Thievery In High Places* speech:

> *I wanted to make sure Members understand that the Federal Reserve Board is not a Federal agency. It is a creature of and responds to the commercial banking system, private, and the way it has worked, its independence, it is totally independent even though*

it was not created from on high...

It is the Federal Reserve Board, even though the Federal Reserve Board is defined in the Federal Reserve Board Act of 1913 as being the fiscal agent of the U.S. Treasury. But it has turned out to be the other way around, and we will go into that in a few minutes with respect to the domestic activities over which we also have little or no control, but on which I have introduced legislation in order to seek protection for the interests of the greatest number in our collective body known as the American society.

As a matter of fact, there are areas of activity that I think the average citizen who reads his Constitution would absolutely conclude that the Committee on Banking, Finance and Urban Affairs of the House had jurisdiction, but it does not. Such things, for instance, as the constitutional mandate, not a privilege, it is a mandate that the Congress control the purse, Treasury; that it also set and determine the value of its coinage or currency, as we say nowadays.

However, that is not really so, through a variety of things that I have discussed on prior occasions and only will sum up; for example, in the matter of affixing the value of the money and coins thereof, that was long abdicated by the Congress after the passage of the Federal Reserve Board Act of 1913 and the creation within the activities of that board of such a thing as the Open Market Committee.

That was structured not unlike the setup of our mother country, England, but today the operations of the Fed are actually of an epoch and an era that no longer reflects the activities in England or Great Britain. For example, it used to be that the Chancellor of the Exchequer could, until actually not too long ago, determine the fall or rise of any cabinet or government in England by just the power to set the value of the bills, of notes, bills, so forth. Unfortunately, today the Federal Reserve, through its Open Market Committee, has that power.

Chapter 9
The American Economy

Our free society was founded upon the principle that each person is a free moral agent with the ability to economically express themselves in our free enterprise system. Although as Americans, we speak proudly of defending our freedom of speech, religion, and other fundamental rights, we rarely speak of defending our economic freedom. This basic freedom is so ingrained into American society, that it is taken for granted. However, be assured, we would quickly notice its absence!

The Free Enterprise System

What is free enterprise? A free enterprise system is one in which (1) the means of production are privately owned and controlled, (2) each person is free to make his own decisions in economic life, and (3) each person's income is roughly in proportion to the benefit society receives for the production of their labor and resources.

How and why it developed... free enterprise was not created by a specific, or deliberate plan. Rather, it emerged as mercantilism, the existing form of economic organization collapsed. Mercantilism is a set of centrally-directed, economic policies forged for the national interests of competing against foreign rivalries. These policies required substantial governmental control over the economic life of the citizens. These controls were exerted in the colonies, as well as, domestically.

The birth of the free enterprise system resulted as a reaction against governmental controls of each individual's economic prosperity. Adam Smith, a Scottish philosopher and economist, presented his concepts of an enterprise system in the *Wealth of Nations*. This book, published in 1776,

greatly aided the development of free enterprise, mainly due
to Smith's central idea of the free enterprise system.

Economic life, as described by Smith's free enterprise system, consisted of society freely producing, exchang-
ing, and consuming goods and services. This process can
only occur after certain *individual* decisions have been made.
Vital decisions, such as, 1) what will be produced and in
what quantities, 2) who is going to produce the desired goods
and services, 3) how will the goods or services be produced,
4) how will the goods or services be distributed, are involved
in a free enterprise system.

We cannot stress enough, how *critical* free and unhindered competition is to the success of the free enterprise
system and our American way of life. However, in the last
century, our federal government has continuously granted
political favors to different sectors of the economy, creating
an unbalanced playing field, so to speak. Unfortunately, when
our federal government *first* granted special privileges to an
industry, it laid the groundwork for other segments of our
economy to point their finger and say: *"The government did
it for them"*.

This political action created a movement to create
equal results through unequal opportunity and the proverbial snowball began rolling down the hill. When does it stop?
When the snow is all gone? When there is no longer a free
economy and our society is no longer free to operate without government interference in every aspect of our lives?

Our business communities must diligently strive to
ensure government is a defender of personal and economic
freedoms. Typically, politicians use the proverbial *big-stick*
of government to restrict freedom in business, attacking the
basic structure of our free society by hindering the natural
forces of supply and demand in our free enterprise economy.

For example, federal farm subsidies have become a
powerful, negative force against the local farmer's economic
survival, giving an unfair advantage to the large multinational agricultural corporations. In addition to their pre-
sumedly, advantageous economies of scale, federal subsidies have contributed to large increases in market share by
these international agricultural conglomerates, enabling them

to underbid the local, unsubsidized farmer's wholesale prices to the distributors and resellers. Thus, taxpayer subsidies unfairly *tip the scales* in favor of these politically-active businesses.

Some may argue: *"That keeps prices lower at the retail level,"* but let us remind you, nothing is free. Would you rather the fair market price be paid by the actual consumer of the product or service, or the actual consumer be allowed to pay less than the natural forces of supply and demand determine, and the American taxpayers (you and I), pay the difference? Remember, our government does not have its *own* money, the American citizens *allow* it to spend our tax revenues, as our elected representatives determine.

Additionally, who do *you* think can best produce quality food products for a market more efficiently: a local farmer, eating the same foods delivered to the market, with their personal pride, property and livelihood at risk, or a large multinational corporation with less-motivated workers and layers of bureaucracy, in conjunction with one of the world's largest bureaucracies, our federal government? Eliminate farm subsidies, allow the local farmer a fighting chance, and let our free market forces determine the survivor.

While the advocates of free enterprise generally blame the federal government, one must be reminded that our government derives its power and direction from us, its citizens. Ultimately, the fate of our liberating, free enterprise system rests squarely on the American citizen's shoulders.

Small business owners, in order to conserve our liberties and continue the promise of unhindered economic opportunities, should utilize their local influence to support politicians who will make community, state, and federal government, a protector of liberty. This is a *critical* requirement to maintaining our economic and personal liberties, and a suggested means for those individuals desiring to positively, affect our nation's future.

Economic Illiteracy

The question remains, with the entire world focused on us: *"Why would Americans allow the economic system that has delivered a much higher standard of living to more people in the last two hundred years than any other system has afforded in the last six thousand years, slip from our grasp?"* The answer to the above-posed question appears to lie in the fact that, apparently, the average citizen, typical politician, and most American business persons, fail to comprehend the several basic ideas inherent in human nature and the free enterprise system. The proponents of that impossible dream, *The Planned Economy*, have failed to realize that the free enterprise system is a natural and unplanned, spontaneous development of human endeavor.

As previously stated, our economic system was not designed, it evolved within the confines of natural economic laws and is controlled by little more than natural human laws. Its moral conscience is governed by Divine law, and documented by our nation's legal system. The free enterprise system is the natural result of a free society, a society that grew out of the settlement and development of a natural world, the continuous evolution of creating needs and consequently, human ingenuity, fulfilling those same needs.

Until the development of this country, the average human lived under primitive conditions, struggling daily to overcome poverty, starvation, disease, slavery or servitude. The early Americans revolted against this order of monarchies and peasants. A new order was implemented, with the Divine Word, both inspiring and guiding them to establish the basic fundamental rights for all mankind, as God-given rights. Each individual is responsible for their own pursuit of happiness, and likewise, accountable for those actions, as well. Incentive then, became the catalyst for production, the primary source of wealth.

Within a few centuries, this order produced the wealthiest, most progressive, most powerful nation in the annals of the history of mankind. Today, this may not seem like such a short time, or a major accomplishment, but consider the previous millenniums. Additionally, a slow, naturally-occurring, random process builds a strong, dynamic foundation which is capable of withstanding great external attacks without losing its sustenance-providing capabilities. As a natural by-product of social, industrial and technological progress, the American free enterprise system provides substantial protection against poverty, disease, and other pre-United States of America woes.

Again, one must ask: *"Why would anyone desire to destroy the proven miracle of a free enterprise system?"* There are several reasons, but the problem is recognized as economic illiteracy. This illiteracy is not limited to the scholastically illiterate, it is shared among the well-educated, as well. It is prevalent on the university campus and common in large segments of the business community. This economic illiteracy is a lack of understanding of the basic fact that the desire to achieve and enjoy the fruits of one's own labor is, as Henry Grady Weaver's book title suggests, *The Mainspring of Human Progress.*

Mankind is motivated by its desire to acquire. Only through enlightenment and the exercise of constraint, does one moderate this primal instinct. However, like it or not, this basic facet of the human personality, is the natural human trait that has given rise to the free enterprise system.

The present situation provides a real philosophical paradox, because few people seriously question the superiority of the free enterprise system, as a producer of wealth. Its superiority is obvious, when we review the last couple centuries of human progress. Yet, the free enterprise system is not secure in today's political climate, because of this economic illiteracy, which we describe.

Economic illiteracy does not imply that Americans are ignorant or incapable of understanding this dynamic system, only that most Americans are not informed of the reasons *why* free enterprise has created such economic advances in our modern age. The trend is to assume that government interference is the solution to most societal ills and generally speaking, many Americans include fundamental economic issues in this category, as well. They fail to understand that the business community is the *ONLY* source of revenue for both individuals and government. Through their resources, businesses provide jobs, economic growth, and continuous, as well as, new wealth for our nation's citizens.

As much as the American people are responsible for defending our economic system, the business community must provide the impetus for leading this crusade to save the miracle of free enterprise. The business sector has the most to lose, the most to gain, and the practical experience within their own respective industries to compete in an open, unhindered free economy.

Trade Protection Measures

Recently, President Bush announced a three-year plan for a 30 % tariff on certain imported steel products, excluding NAFTA members and certain developing countries. This move is certainly appreciated by the domestic steel industry, which had launched recent extensive television campaigns to supplement their lobbyists' efforts. President Bush probably considered the political risks associated with not following through on locally-televised reruns of his recent presidential campaign speech promising support for the bankrupt American steel industry. Although, in the president's defense, there are legitimate national defense interests involved in this decision, as well. If Americans allowed our country's steel industry to become nonexistent, forcing our nation to be completely dependent upon imported steel, there could be serious implications in the event of a serious military conflict, or worldwide trade wars.

However, the United States must be prepared for retaliation by other trading nations on other American industries, such as agriculture, technology, etc... Consequently, will there be an escalation of trade barriers to the point of actual trade wars? It's easy to understand the temptation for continued government interference; but are free trade obstacles the solution? Are we only masking the problems and postponing *real* solutions? As most, this latest government interference in free trade was initially designed as a temporary measure. Hopefully, it will be short-lived and allow our domestic steel industry sufficient time to address the real issues of long-term survivability, such as pensions, capital investment requirements, and evolving customer demands.

Last August, the Bush administration also enacted a 19.3 % import tariff on Canadian softwood lumber, which critics claim will harm the American consumers by creating product shortages. On August 22, 2001, CBC News reported, Canadian Prime Minister Jean Chretien:

> *Paraphrasing his talk with Bush, Chretien said he asked the president, "You want gas, you want oil and you don't want wood? It's too bad, but if you have free trade, you have free trade."*

Foreign trade policies which hinder the forces of free trade are not the solution to American problems. The advocates of tariffs are seeking self-serving interests at the American taxpayers and consumers' expense. A hypocritical foreign trade policy will only undermine American foreign interests and lessen our moral credibility as the world's leader and proponent of free trade.

It is quite disconcerting to observe a possible trend of protectionist measures by a self-proclaimed, conservative president. President Bush must not succumb to domestic industry pressures, or campaign supporters' interests at the *expense* of the American citizens. The concept of free trade is profoundly simple, *free trade.*

Additionally, when considering the United States' past trade-protectionist measures' effects on the world's trading nations, this time we are prompted to quote an excerpt from Frederic Bastiat's *The Law,* written in 1850:

> *In virtue of the principle of universal justice, no citizen being able to prevent another citizen from buying or selling abroad, the commercial relations of this nation will be free and widespread. No one will deny that these relations contribute to the maintenance of peace. They will themselves constitute a veritable and precious system of defense, which will render arsenals, fortified places, navies, and standing armies well-nigh useless.*

With the defense budget skyrocketing due to the American *War on Terrorism*, and as the current and future American taxpayers are being forced to pay for *policing* the world, unrestricted foreign trade might be an investment consideration. Would we rather invest domestically, bolstering our economic capabilities to compete unhindered on a worldwide basis, or continue to spend American dollars abroad on foreign governments in hopes of their country pursuing American interests? Abraham Lincoln once stated:

> *Am I not destroying my enemies when I make friends of them?*

Doesn't it make sense that if we create strong free economic trading relationships with other countries, that the same human traits that motivate Americans to self-fulfilling behavior, will motivate them, as well? Free trade impediments contribute to ill-willed, nationalistic sentiments, instead of humanity's natural inclination for the pursuit of individual interests, which in turn, benefits all parties involved in a free-trade transaction.

Certainly, there are situations which arise that require our government's negotiations, in order to protect against the illegal dumping of foreign goods; however, that should be done through the legislative process, in lieu of presidential executive orders. It is the responsibility of Congress to determine the responsible and proper course of action.

The world is weary of American double-standards. Our government generously subsidizes agricultural production, creating a system which rewards overproduction. This, in turn, gluts the world markets with American subsidized grains, etc... which drives down global agricultural prices. In turn, agricultural nations are forced to seek American charity, which is another burden on the American taxpayer.

Therefore, our nation's agricultural subsidies are simply, another form of special interest groups obtaining political favors, at the taxpayer's expense. Additionally, the American government-subsidized grain for sale on world markets, is *exactly* what our government defines as *dumping*. We are a perfect example of, *Do as I say, not as I do*. Our hypocritical world trade policies will inevitably, become a worldwide *war chant*, either economically, or militarily, possibly both, against the United States of America.

America will only *gain* economic strength by pursuing a broad open-trade policy, but as any successful business person can attest, it will not be without difficulties and hardships. The trade barriers suggest a less painful, immediate solution; however, we are only raising the dam without reducing, and even possibly increasing, the flow of anti-American sentiments. Inevitably, the consequences will overflow onto the heartlands of America.

As the world's staunchest advocate of free enterprise and trade, America does not have the luxury of *choosing* which industries, products, or nations, receive the blessing of diverted American taxpayer revenue. We can not advocate free enterprise and free trade, EXCEPT... This is the hypocrisy the world views when America demands unhindered market access, while enacting import trade barriers. Our federal government should carefully extract itself from all economic interference, including import tariffs, market subsidies, and suppressive labor policies.

Granted, this will be a *distasteful* pill to swallow, but we have created the illness, and we should be the ones to pay the price for regaining our economic and personal freedoms. Our children should inherit a nation positioned for even greater achievements in the next millennium, not an ailing nation adrift in the mire of liberal politics and decreasing individual economic opportunity and freedoms.

Big Business And Big Problems

Much is needed to affect a proper restoration of our nation. The attack against the free enterprise system is not so much being won by its adversaries, as much as, it is being lost by its advocates. For what conceivable reason does the small-business community refuse to defend itself? There are many possible reasons for this lack of action, with some of the more probable being:

1) Preoccupation with business matters is primarily a trait of small-business owners, however, large corporations suffer from this ailment, as well. The business community strives to operate as efficiently as possible, to ensure the exchange of wealth for

its products and/or services. Likewise, the competitive nature of America's business environment discourages unilateral investment of resources in a *perceived* nonessential area of concern.

2) Narrowly-focused trade associations pursue self-serving interests without considering broad implications on society, as a whole. In other words, an *every person for himself* attitude is prevalent. Even still, a *country* perspective may resemble, *Every hog's so busy at the trough, there's no time to worry about the other pigs, or when the slop will run out!*

3) Business consolidations are creating a temporary, false sense of survivability and prosperity in the face of ever-increasing regulations and tax codes. The efficiencies gained by technology and scale will eventually flatten or retract. Coupled with excessive government interference, long-term, many of these consolidations may result in failed ventures. Meanwhile, most investors are complacent about the continuous growth of government and its escalating costs.

4) In spite of individual small-business efforts, their interests are not being protected by their elected representatives because well-funded, special-interest groups are lobbying these same Congressional representatives with generous campaign contributions, tickets to the Super Bowl, World Series, or NBA playoffs, and free flights to their favorite vacation spot.

5) There is a lack of a clear and concise understanding of the challenges they face, thus they have no specific solution or plan of action, except to perhaps, work a little harder, a little longer, and a little smarter. They struggle daily to merely survive under a wide array of government-imposed burdens.

One of our concerns, with the intrusion of government regulations and the more than fifty-percent tax load on individual small-business owners, when accounting for both employee and employer contributions of federal, state, Social Security, Medicare, unemployment payroll taxes, both personal and business property taxes, fuel taxes, telecommunication surcharges... ad nauseam, will any businesses survive other than large multinational corporations that have no patriotic loyalty to America and singularly serve the financial interests of their shareholders with no conscience for employees, community, nation or humanity?

Consequently, when there are only a few mega-corporations controlling *all* business and commerce, where will the competition be? Sure, there are antitrust laws, but have you ever noticed when there are two gas stations on a corner? Typically, the gas stations will have different fuel sources, different expenses, different ownership and different management, but both, individually, come to the same retail price conclusion? Is that collusion or market forces at work in a limited-competition environment?

This cozy, limited-competition environment will only necessitate more government regulations to protect its citizens, requiring more taxes to pay for these additional government services, furthering the growth of government to the further demise and hindrance of small-business, which is the manifestation of American entrepreneurship and our way of life. With limited competition, large conglomerates will simply pass this costs on to consumers, furthering the advance of corporate America's stranglehold on our nation and lowering the average American's standard of living, while corporate profits continue to be tallied elsewhere around the world.

The irony of such a devastating cycle, if continued, is there will not be an adequate source of taxable income sufficient to pay for the rising costs of government. Indeed, this is true today. Our government has outgrown the American citizens' ability to pay for its expenses, as our elected representatives *continue* to outspend their revenue.

However, prior to a catastrophic collapse of our free enterprise system and the complete loss of our personal and economic freedoms, our federal government using the full-strength of the American citizens' credit, our war machine, and billion dollar foreign-aid budgets, will have opened sufficient developing nations' markets, granting American capitalists safe havens in their global expansion efforts. Our government's foreign policy, is deliberately and without conscience, facilitating corporate America's global expansion at the American worker and taxpayer's expense.

These global corporations will share no American patriotic responsibility with their employees. Thomas Jefferson with uncanny foresight:

> *I hope we shall crush in its birth the aristocracy of our moneyed corporations, which dare already to challenge our government to a trial of strength and bid defiance to the laws of our country.*

Will big business use our government to stifle the American people's desire and ability to generate a tolerable life-style against the forces of wage-suppression, ever-increasing tax loads, unemployment, and overregulation of free enterprise?

Will the bureaucrats and corporate executives, with their unrestrained access to government policy, avoid an impending American economic stagnation? With telecommunications and personal financial capability to reside anywhere in the world, many Americans own foreign property, or have built self-sustaining, secure dwellings in this nation. With little incentive to halt the looting of the American taxpayers' pockets, the stark reality of an aristocracy isolated from the *common* people, controlling their economic futures, is not a science-fiction scene, but a glaring possibility.

Our military and paramilitary organizations routinely perform exercises in riot-control and other civil suppression acts. If our government's unrefutable legal authority and accompanying power of enforcement is perceived as an available tool, allowing our nation's business and political leaders to selfishly pursue personal interests to the detriment of American society, there will be little conscience to struggle with the innate human temptations of greed. Unfortunately, with the most technologically-advanced and best-trained military in the world, the American citizens would have few choices, other than capitulation.

As the great American theologian and philosopher Dr. Reinhold Niebuhr observed in his book, *Moral Man and Immoral Society*:

> *Politics will to the end of history, be an area where conscience and power meet, where the ethical and coercive factors of human life will interpenetrate and work out their tentative and uneasy compromises. The democratic method of resolving social conflict, which some romanticists hail as a triumph of the ethical over the coercive factor, is really much more coercive than at first seems apparent. The majority has its way, not because the minority believes that the majority is right (few minorities are willing to grant the majority the moral prestige of such a concession), but because the votes of the majority are a symbol of its social strength. Whenever a minority believes that it has some strategic advantage which outweighs the power of numbers, and whenever it is sufficiently intent upon its ends, or desperate enough about its position in society, it refuses to accept the dictates of the majority.*

Dr. Niebuhr obviously understood the intended *majority rule* premise for a self-governing, democratic nation; however his insightful observation of the possibility for a *minority rule* within a democratic, self-governing nation is more astute.

He aptly describes the circumstances in modern America. The wealthy and those aspiring great wealth desire to no longer abide by the same laws as other Americans. They choose to influence our lawmakers to gain benefits for themselves, which contrastively, as a fundamental law of physics states, "*For every action there is an equal and opposite reaction*", negatively affects the American citizens. The wealthy's generous efforts of persuasion quickly gain acceptance by our legislators' personal greed.

Today, it is common for our nation's lawmakers to

use *double-talk* for the titles of their craftily-articulated legislation to prevent their constituents from understanding the true consequences of their actions with only a casual observation. Our legislators' devises gain their benefactors carefully-calculated, economic advantages once legalized, while the corrupt legislators and bureaucrats are paid with money, *legally embezzled* from our nation's citizens and taxpayers.

The recent Enron scandal has stimulated widespread discussions on the accounting methods of corporate America. This is a positive result of a negative situation; however, currently, there is a national shareholders' association that is lobbying our federal government, spelled T-A-X-P-A-Y-E-R, to administer the independent auditing of these corporate accountants. Surely, the same shareholders that freely allow their board of directors to spend corporate profits on staggering bonuses and equity options for upper management, will support their corporation paying for its own expense of independent audits on corporate balance sheets.

Hopefully, our conservative stalwarts in the Congress and Senate will not allow the additional burdening of American taxpayers by creating yet, another layer of bureaucracy. Are they claiming there is not *one* independent auditing firm trustworthy? This is a perfect example of a special-interest group lobbying our politicians to gain political favor, while expecting *all* Americans to bankroll their personal interests.

Is it then, too late? Has socialism, or some new socioeconomic hybrid already advanced beyond our ability to defend our ailing free enterprise system? Has corporate America become institutionalized to the point of inseparable bedfellows with our federal government? Has America's large global corporations sank their roots into the life energy of this nation and our government to the point of being in absolute control of their corporate well-being at the expense of the American public? Do the relatively few majority shareholders of a handful of Fortune 100 corporations wield more power than our politicians dare face?

This life or death struggle for the American way of life and our individual economic freedom demands your efforts. For clarification, we do not propose more legislation to correct this liberal, downward course. We challenge the status quo to compete for their livelihood on an *equal* basis with all Americans and the world. Throughout history, it has *always* been the case, whereas the privileged erect barriers to prevent loss by designing systemic advantages for *existing* prosperity. Their fear of loss motivates their guilt-ridden consciences to instill a sense of Divine justification for their actions, and consequently, some truly believe they are uniquely, worthy of privileged luxury.

Will these manipulations of our nation's commerce laws be allowed to continue unchecked? They will, unless you choose to become involved in your local, state, and federal elections, stop ignoring your civic responsibilities, and demand accountability of your elected representatives.

In a 1996 interview with Alejandro Benes, our favorite liberal scholar, Dr. Arthur Schlesinger, Jr., is quoted:

> *(Schlesinger argues)... that despite the lapses of the national government, it is self-deluding to believe that power taken from the federal government will end up anywhere but in the hands of corporations. He adds that the only balance to "private and unaccountable" economic power is the power of the national government.*

Quite to the contrary, the supreme economic power lies in the free market forces of an unhindered free enterprise system. We agree that there is a problem with unaccountable economic power in the form of billion dollar corporations, however, we highly disagree on the proposed solution. Dr. Schlesinger argues for increasing power to the federal government to regulate this problem, whereas, we believe there is already too much economic interference by the federal government's plethora of laws designed to *fix* society, which have inadvertently, created the chronic imbalance between labor and management, originally.

If left intact, the free market's supply and demand of all commodities, including labor, are an equalizing force. As we later address our nation's liberal immigration policies, we will forego any discussion on the topic, at this time. However, the powerful influence big business exerts on our elected representatives is undeniable, and only through the electorate process can we address this issue without further erosion of individual economic opportunities.

The fight for survival of the free enterprise system is continuing: to win the war will require a determined, organized campaign for educating the uninformed, the one factor which allows false doctrines to empower their proponents. If the American small-business community will commit its tremendous intellectual, financial, numerical and organizational strength to a positive, self-educating program, and exert *their* influences to elect conservative politicians, liberals would lose their strongest social-reforming tool, political favors. No politician could be elected to office without the majority support of a politically-active, small-business constituency.

If you recall our definition of *liberal*, you may more fully understand the threat of their politics of *change*. Conservatives comprehend and appreciate the Divine genius in the mechanics of the free enterprise system and defend its integrity. As liberals slowly erode the base, passing unjust laws that restrict the flow of free-market forces, they are gradually creating the demise of our nation's economic freedom, thus our personal freedoms. The irony of this tragedy strikes deep into the heart of the business community, which is the major source of funding for the liberal politicians dismantling the American business infrastructure.

Our leaders must deliberately and methodically, rescind the past century's unjust legislation. It will require great contemplation, compassion, and commitment, but nonetheless, it must be done. It is essential that we return our nation to the free market principles that are the manifestation of the eternal truths of humanity, those maxims that evoke our heritage, preserve our present strength, and guarantee our future survival in the most inspirational light of the human spirit.

Since our usage of the term, *unjust laws* may seem ambiguous, it may be helpful to convey our interpretation by once again using the words of an imprisoned Dr. Martin Luther King Jr.:

An unjust law is a code that a minority inflicts on a

majority that is not binding on itself. This is differ-
ence made legal. A just law is a code that a major-
ity compels a minority to follow that it is willing
to follow itself. This is sameness made legal.

Although Dr. King was obviously addressing civil rights, the application of injustice to the American citizens through economic advantages for special-interest groups, is equally, unjust. Economically, the majority suffer when unfair advantages are granted to a minority. Must we feel hunger pains, or be left homeless, before we realize the *injustice* of these threats on our ability to pursue happiness and prosperity? As Dr. King continues:

There comes a time when the cup of endurance
runs over and men are no longer willing to be
plunged into an abyss of injustice where they
experience the blackness of corroding despair.

As surely as time marches forward, without our increased participation in the business of our nation, there will come a day when the economic injustices America's liberal political leaders, international financiers, and global corporations conspire to implement, are as painful to the majority of Americans as the sting of a master's whip on the backs of slaves. History reveals the suffering and severity of personal and economic hardships that result from the emotional and desperate actions of civil disobediences and violent political revolutions. We must act to remove the burdensome weight of special-interest groups' agendas via government interference in our private lives, our businesses, and our pursuit of happiness.

As one ponders the many difficulties our nation faces, it becomes evident that a contributing source of additional misery, is due to *We the People,* not being in full command of our government. It is time for the American citizens to regain their authority as the masters of their own destiny. If we wait until the symptoms are intolerable before we take action, the medicine will be much more distasteful and a cure much more difficult to obtain.

Chapter 10

The Squandering Of Freedom

Our society is the living proof of our nation's materialistic success. We have advanced in the area of material wealth to a level never achieved by any other nation in history. However, this newly-found, material wealth has generated new problems of its own. These problems have resolved themselves in a pattern of failure, because we have not... and are not, willing to realistically, face them.

This is an age of softness when people are saying: *"Harmony at any price"* and *"Let the government do it"*. We are immersed in our comforts and luxuries, oblivious to the dangers surrounding us. As evidenced by the majority of Americans' behavior, an argument could be made that many Americans are politically lazy, self-centered, and are intoxicated with the abundance of easily-accessible entertainment and diversions that are proliferating in our society.

We have created big government by our accepting attitude toward the *bait* of socialism, basically, *something-for-nothing*, in an era when idleness has become profitable and the rewards for productivity are declining. Big government continuously increases taxes, which ultimately, are imposed upon earnings, while subsidies are offered for failure.

In his promotion of an ever-growing, federal government, Dr. Arthur M. Schlesinger Jr., interviewed by journalist, Alejandro Benes, in *The Guardian of Liberalism,* in all his liberal glory, states:

> *I think it's an illusion to think that the government closer to the people is more responsive to the people... Most of the progress in making this a more decent country has come through the*

national government, not through local government.

We squander our priceless heritage, carelessly. We are impoverishing future generations with a legacy of big government, monumental debt, and lessening economic opportunities. How is this *justifiable?*

For example, the Inspector General's report contained within House Report 104-861, dated September 28, 1996, on the Department of Energy, a federal government agency spiraling out of control, far beyond the scope of the original intent of the department's sponsors:

The Department of Energy (DOE) budget for fiscal year 1996 was $15.9 billion, and DOE had a total of 18,743 employees. As management issues are reviewed within the DOE, there is a need to re-examine the Department's basic missions. Created in 1977 to respond to the Nation's energy crisis, DOE's priorities have shifted dramatically, first to nuclear weapons production in the 1980s and then to environmental cleanup today. DOE now is approaching new or expanded missions in such areas as industrial competitiveness, science education, safety and health, and nuclear arms and verification. Many experts believe that DOE needs to concentrate more on energy-related missions, such as energy policy, energy information, and energy supply research and development and that many of its remaining missions should be moved elsewhere.

Notwithstanding the broad range of expert opinion that a fundamental rethinking of DOE's missions is needed, the Department has shown little interest in reviewing its missions or reforming its management practices. The Department's own "strategic plan" clings to the status quo by assuming that all of DOE's current missions are valid and should remain within the Department. Likewise, as discussed later in this report, DOE has failed to provide its national laboratories with sorely needed guidance on what their missions should be. DOE also has been reluctant to reform its management practices. This is particularly unfortunate because its serious management problems are many.

This is not an attempt to beleaguer individuals responsible for the creation, or present administration of the Department of Energy, just an observation of an unbiased review by our government's Inspector General's office, a fellow government agency.

Do we choose to ignore such a scathing report by the General Accounting Office (GAO) on a federal agency that is mismanaged, misguided, and consuming billions of taxpayer dollars? Unfortunately, this is just a small portion of the problems within the expanding federal bureaucracy of our nation's government. A very alarming statement also contained in the GAO's report to the 104th Congress follows:

The Government Reform and Oversight Committee's review has revealed that the alarming problems of mismanagement, waste and abuse in Federal departments and agencies persist and may be growing. For example, an update of the twelve "worst examples of government waste" cited in the Government Operations Committee's 1992 staff report indicates that only one of the twelve examples has shown significant improvement. Seven of the cited examples are worse now, and three of these are much worse.

It is a tribute to our government and its system of checks and balances that enables individual American taxpayers to have accessibility to these reports. However, it is up to each of us, to choose 1) to find the report, 2) read and comprehend it, 3) make the effort to find a solution. If each American would do just that much, our nation would be overwhelmed by the progress that could be made in such a short time.

Our federal government, mired in political appointments, overlapping authority, disjointed efforts, and a myriad of other problems common to a *centralized federal government,* has overextended its responsibilities, authority, and capabilities. But please, don't take *our* word, the GAO report to the 104th Congress continues:

> *1) Only 8 percent of callers could reach the Internal Revenue Service by phone for the tax year of 1995. The rate has plummeted since the 1989 tax filing season, when the agency answered 58 per - cent of its telephone calls for assistance.*
> *2) Drug use among teens doubled during the past four years. Spending on drug treatment programs tripled since 1988, but the estimated number of individuals treated actually declined. 80 percent of users are not enrolled in treatment programs, many of those casual users are teens.*
> *3) The Department of Interior "paid" $800,015 for a $150 vacuum cleaner, $700,035 for a $350 dishwasher, and $79 million for a $793 mobile radio unit. (See page 123 of the GAO report)*
> *4) $1.6 million was paid by the Department of Interior for "personality profiles" for agency supervisors and the agency is considering expanding the program to all 15,000 agency employees.*
> *5) If the IRS were a taxpayer, it would be audited. Total amounts of tax revenue and tax refunds it collects cannot be verified.*
> *6) $12.6 million is being taken out of the Social Security Trust Funds to pay Federal employees to work full-time on union activities. One such employee is paid $81,000 per year and performs no work for the agency. More than 1,800 Federal employees are spending part of their time on union activities at the Social Security Administration.*
> *7) The Environmental Protection Agency (EPA) reduced its total advisory committees, but increased the amount they spend on them by 84 percent. Only 6 committees were required by law; the EPA has 22 advisory committees.*
> *8) The Department of Labor has been tolerating*

the use of fraudulent wage data for purposes of the Davis-Bacon Act, potentially inflating Federal and State construction, alteration and repair costs by hundreds of millions of dollars.

9) At the Department of Agriculture, an estimated $2 billion per year in overpayments in the Food Stamp program are never recovered. A large quantity of food stamps are used in trafficking for non-food items, such as drugs and guns.

10) The Immigration and Naturalization Service spends $30 million annually for overtime. Under its pay system, the agency can and does pay for 16 hours of overtime for as little as 1 hour of work on Sundays and holidays, and it even pays workers overtime to take annual leave.

11) The Department of the Interior failed to collect as much as $1.2 billion in payments on oil royalties, and in California alone, oil companies were undercharged as much as $856 million for royalty rights.

12) The estimated cost of fraud and abuse this year to the Department of Health and Human Services Medicare and Medicaid programs may reach $26.9 billion.

13) 163 Federal job training programs costing more than $20 billion compete against one another to serve the same client populations, and have overlapping and conflicting administrative structures.

14) The Department of Agriculture allowed Federal prisoners to make long-distance telephone calls to sex and adult party lines at its expense.

15) Federal employees at the Department of Commerce have used Government credit cards to make purchases of liquor, jewelry, flowers, music, payment of on-line computer services and private auto insurance.

Are you *furious,* yet? Unfortunately, in *Late Night* style, our Top Ten list is not only ten, or even necessarily, the *Top Ten.* These are randomly selected examples of our federal bureaucracy's waste. For those readers that are still not motivated to action, please read the complete report by the GAO at the following web address:

www.house.gov/reform/reports/govmang.htm

What will it *take* to make Americans pay attention? When will we draw the line on the systemic wastes of a federal bureaucracy, which by its very nature, is incapable of producing any other outcome? Is a penny saved, not a penny earned? Would *you* like a raise? All that is required, is for every American to become involved in their nation's business. It doesn't require monumental acts of heroism, or risks to life and limb. However, inaction *does* run the risk of losing our liberty, which would be far more painful and enduring than any physical injury. It only requires voters to fulfill their patriotic responsibility... something people in other countries, and American patriots in our nation's past, have died for, the *right* to VOTE.

Let us clarify, we are not pointing fingers, as when we point one finger, there are three pointing back at us. It is not any one person's fault. Our founding fathers understood the weaknesses of human nature and painstakingly, with great reverence and forethought, designed a system of governing a nation that compatibly merged sinful human nature with the checks and balances of our federal government and specifically limited its powers, leaving all remaining authority to the citizens, and their respective states.

Our continuing personal and economic freedoms are contingent upon our embracing acceptance of certain responsibilities. To shirk these responsibilities and leave the business of our country in the hands of *We the Politicians, We the Labor Union Bosses,* and *We the Special-Interest Groups,* should cause no surprise as we see the direction of government veer off course, to the detriment of *We the People.*

When our government went into receivership after President Roosevelt declared our nation bankrupt, our republic, our Constitution, and our sovereignty was surrendered. Instead of the God-given rights represented in the original Constitution, the resulting democracy protects and enforces the desires of the majority, unless the majority is silent, which in America is a cliche; then the government upholds the manipulations of the few, the powerful, and the wealthy, whom engage in persuasive tactics aimed at *our* elected representatives.

It is with great anticipation that we consider the implications of the McCain-Feingold Campaign Reform Bill, which originated in the United States Senate and President Bush recently signed into law. This is a heroic effort by the sponsors of the bill, and a monumentally, historical vote in our Senate. We are hopeful this indicates a return of patriotism to our lawmakers and our nation's capital.

The elimination of *soft money*, which allowed the unlimited raising of campaign funds by the political parties, will drastically reduce the influence our nation's wealthy can freely exercise upon our nation's political future. Although the McCain-Feingold bill *did* raise individual contribution levels, their limits remain reasonable, compared to the staggering amounts of *soft money* contributions, previously allowed.

Campaign reform is essential to creating a political environment that upholds the concept of *one vote, one equal voice* in our nation's political affairs. Prior to the campaign reform bill passage, wealthy individuals openly funneled enormous amounts of *political persuasion* through the political parties to the most agreeable candidates. There are still political fund-raising dinners, which generate millions of dollars for campaign contributions. However, it is encouraging that our elected officials have finally taken an acknowledging, first-step in campaign reform.

Unfortunately, the Federal Election Commission (FEC) is responsible for enforcing the newly-enacted campaign reforms. The FEC consists of three Republicans and three Democrats, which are political appointees. These appointees are responsible for enforcing campaign infractions committed by those individuals that have the power over their appointment.

Additionally, there is a partisan effort to replace the

Federal Election *Commission* with a single *individual* political appointee, consolidating enforcement authority into *one* politically-appointed individual. Furthermore, special-interest groups have filed legal briefs challenging the constitutionality of the McCain-Feingold Bill, which will ultimately be heard by a politically-appointed Supreme Court.

In President Ronald Reagan's autobiography, *An American Life*, he revealed:

> *Too often, in my experience, Congress reminds us that it is a political organism. The central preoccupation of too many of its members is getting reelected; too often, instead of legislative statesmanship, this produces cynical posturing and pandering to the campaign contributors that have the fattest wallets.*

The active participation of all Americans in determining the future of our nation is essential. We must not allow the special-interest groups' unhampered access to our nation's lawmakers to continue. As long as there are political favors to be gained, such as, government contracts and business favorable legislation, the motivation for big business to devise various means of rewarding liberal politicians that are either knowingly or unknowingly destroying our free enterprise system, will remain. Therefore, we are hesitant to consider that creative and novel approaches to the influencing of our politicians will not be forthcoming, either through self-serving legislation, or mutually-motivated attempts at exploiting legal loopholes, even if a) the campaign reform legislation is upheld in court, b) the notoriously, ineffective FEC survives its commission status and *responsibly* performs its duties.

Consider Dr. Martin Luther King Jr.'s response to the Birmingham clergymen's criticism on April 16, 1963, written on the margins of newspapers from a Birmingham jail cell:

> *History is the long and tragic story of the fact that privileged groups seldom give up their privileges*

*voluntarily. Individuals may see the moral light
and voluntarily give up their unjust posture; but as
Reinhold Niebuhr has reminded us, groups are
more immoral than individuals.*

Our Constitution's authors could never have imagined in their wildest dreams, the apathy of the typical, disinterested American citizen in the affairs of their country. Remember the old adage, *"The squeaky wheel gets the grease."* This proverb applies to our nation's business, as well.

There is a simple concept at work in our nation's government... lobbyists lobby, politicians politicize, and voters vote. What we are neglecting in the dynamics of our nation's political realm, are the empowering voters. The voters are *NOT* voting! We are neglecting our responsibility to ourselves, our children and our nation.

Let your elected representative know if you approve or disapprove of their actions, by voting. If an incumbent is not reelected because of supporting a position counter to the majority of their constituency's interests, would that send a message to the newly-elected representative, concerning that particular issue, as well as, voter accountability?

Are we witnessing the fulfillment of Jefferson's warning? He cautioned his fellow statesman:

*If once people become inattentive to the public
affairs, you and I, Congress and Assemblies,
Judges, and Governors, shall become wolves.*

Some politicians are surely wolves, or at least, they act like them, when it comes to reelection. Consequently, the American voters must become vigil, standing guard over the *hen house*, lest we go hungry.

When politicians are in control of government, they will pass unjust laws contrary to the will of the people and contrary to the general public's interest. Often, special-interest groups gain political favors by enticing politicians with personal benefits in the form of consulting jobs, honorarium, employment for relatives, generous campaign contributions, or even contributions to their favorite charities, i.e. their children's college fund, etc. Other times, special-interest groups appeal to a politician's sense of decency and portray their cause as *patriotic* or *justified*. However, often times the *not-so-obvious* consequences are overlooked with little research, due to the overabundance of difficult issues facing our representatives.

These actions permit the voice of the minority to be heard while the promises of *responsible* solutions to the majority are forgotten. Many significant examples of our *misplaced trust* exist today. It is doubtful that even *one* state would have a majority vote for busing of school children, yet, busing exists. Likewise, it is highly doubtful that popular vote would prohibit prayer at extracurricular school activities; however, our federal government has banned its presence.

What *should* be highly-controversial and considered a morally criminal act by our federal government is buried in the depths of our nation's business. Public Law 107-25, signed into law on August 13, 2001, is another seemingly, benign example of taxpayer subsidies for primarily, our nation's corporate agricultural producers. It is not the fact that $4.62 billion of taxpayer money is delivered into corporate coffers that is so bothersome, but Sec. 4 (a) authorizes our federal government to spend *our* tax dollars to pay tobacco producers $129 million under section 204 (b) of the Agricultural Risk Protection Act of 2000, (Public Law 106-224; 7 U.S.C. 1421 note).

It is with great hypocrisy that our federal government subsidizes the production of tobacco, while simultaneously, raising user taxes on the product to supposedly, discourage smokers. Is it possible that our government is more interested in politically-acceptable forms of tax revenue, than the well-being of its citizens?

According to RJ Reynolds, American citizens have paid an *additional* $127.1 billion in taxes, for using a product which is legal. Additionally, tobacco companies have committed $246 billion over the next twenty-five years, to fund state programs. Although wholesale prices have increased dramatically, RJ Reynolds claims the government receives 9 times more profit from the sale of cigarettes than it does *manufacturing* them.

The bottom-line results of the cigarette tax appears to transfer capital from the American citizens to the tobacco growers receiving political favor, rather than the choices of our free market economy, with the remainder consumed by our spendthrift legislators. We are not smokers and do not advocate on their behalf. However, our government's behavior, regarding the *sin* taxes, is ludicrous and hypocritical, at best. Government is not the individual's conscience; nor should it be our nation's.

Another little-discussed issue, which we believe is in conflict with the majority's interests and desires. Puerto Rico, as a commonwealth, is allowed to grant U.S. corporations federal tax exemption, while simultaneously, offering the protection and security of the United States government. Furthermore, the Puerto Rican citizens are given statutory American citizenship status, without the requirements and burden of a federal income tax.

Yes, it is true that American citizens from Puerto Rico receive slightly, reduced federal benefits and are prohibited from voting in presidential elections, but since approximately two-thirds of all eligible American voters do not participate in the presidential elections, we question the percentage of those Americans which would choose between federal income tax and their inability to vote in presidential elections.

America's nonvoting, non-taxpaying statutory citizens are allowed to live in America and enjoy the benefits of personal and economic liberties, without the accompanying responsibility. Additionally, the Puerto Rican federal government promotes individual economic advancements for its citizens, as well as, all Hispanics in this country.

With only slightly less Puerto Rican citizens living in the United States than those residing on the island, clearly, the Puerto Rican citizens have embraced their taxpaying fellow American citizens, as neighbors. The following is an excerpt from the Puerto Rico Federal Affairs Administration's press releases via their website, www.prfaa.com:

According to the Puerto Rico Federal Affairs

Administration (PRFAA) announcement on July 7, 2001, attorney and activist Luis R. Pastrana Silva has been named the new director of its Central Florida regional office. Based in Orlando, PRFAA's Central Florida regional office is charged with advocating for the social and economic empowerment of Puerto Ricans, and all Hispanics across the U.S., while providing access to resources and information for the local community. "The latest census shows that nearly half of all Puerto Ricans reside on the mainland, and Florida is the second largest area of concentration. PRFAA's mission is to enfranchise and serve not only those Puerto Ricans on the island, but also our many communities across the country," said Pastrana.

Most Americans don't realize that our nation allows this *special* relationship with the citizens of U.S. territories. Does one question the reason the citizens of our territories continue to vote against statehood? *Why buy the cow, if the milk is free?* The American citizens should demand their territorial brothers and sisters *ante up* and equally share the financial burden of freedom.

Furthermore, in addition to the Puerto Rican statutory citizens not paying federal income tax, their own government strives to promote their special interests. Is this another case of the American taxpayers subsidizing the benefits of a special-interest group? Perhaps the definition of special-interest group is becoming more focused. It is not only industry, labor, environmentalists, etc., but is, as diverse as the United States of America.

The PRFAA press release continued:

As Central Florida Regional Director, Pastrana will work with local, regional and statewide elected officials, corporations and community-based organizations to partner on a wide range of educational and advocacy projects on behalf of Puerto Ricans. The Central Florida office is also staffed with a Community Outreach coordinator and administrative personnel who can assist the community with information about basic government services such as birth certificates, social security questions, drivers license and voter registration information.

We have no complaint against our fellow Puerto Rican citizens, it is only human nature to accept *having your cake and eat it, too*, if offered, spoon-fed with glowing candles. However, the remainder of our nation's citizens should be conscious of our taxpayer subsidy and determine its acceptability or not.

A final example, a minority fraction of Americans were in favor of relinquishing the Panama Canal, yet our government turned over control and possession of the Panama Canal to the Panamanian government, which has allowed a publicly-owned entity, the Panama Canal Authority, to operate the canal since 1999. Our release of the Panama Canal was during a crucial time, due to the shortage of fresh water. CNN reported on November 1, 2000, that the Panama canal required 52 million gallons of water to float each ship through the canal. Due to the deforestation of Panama, sediment and biological blooms are prevalent throughout the canal system, causing increased maintenance problems.

Our concern is that a publicly-owned, foreign entity that is possibly struggling to continue its daily operations, due to greatly increased maintenance costs, is much more vulnerable to hostile takeovers and outside interests. Additionally, if proper maintenance is neglected and the strategic waterway is allowed to deteriorate to minimally-acceptable levels of operation, are we prepared for the consequences of an inoperable Panama Canal in the event of a major military conflict on either side of the continent?

Although treaties exist which guarantee a neutral zone, even in war time, without American administration, security and oversight to maintain capacity and eliminate or at least, minimize the threat of sabotage, we have once again added another straw against the backbone of our freedoms. Which straw will be the last? Hopefully, that question will remain unanswered. However, a future with circumstances unforeseen, could prove releasing the Panama Canal was a fatal error in the protection of our national interests.

In spite of all our challenges to overcome, the United States of America is still the greatest nation on earth. Many people believe this is due to the climate, natural resources, geographical location, etc. These factors however, are infinitesimal, relative to the primary cause and source of our nation's greatness. It is our superior system of government which allows the human spirit to burgeon without limitations that has protected the birth, growth, and likewise, the stagnation of our country. Nonetheless, it is a finite source of power, and if we do not strengthen our nation with our own energy and efforts, it too, will fail.

If we do not stop relinquishing our personal and economic freedoms to our government for sale to the highest bidder, we face a national crisis. Step-by-step, we are losing our freedoms so gradually that we won't even be aware, until it finally extinguishes our desire for life, liberty, and happiness. The formidable task of regaining our personal and economic freedoms will require each and every American to share in the awesome responsibility of ensuring our children a reasonable prospect of economic prosperity.

Finally, after eight long years, we have a new president and administration with whom we may not always agree; however, he is restoring character and integrity in the highest office in the land. Each of us that voted and participated in the process, regardless to whom that vote was cast, can take great pride in the fact that we have determined it was time to make a change. Our acknowledgment of the moral decline in our nation's government was the first step down the path of restoring our personal freedoms.

We, as a moral society, will have overwhelming success working together for a peaceful solution to our nation's problems, if we choose to *pick up our cross*.We must devote our lives to the mind of Christ to succeed at anything in life. This time-tested philosophy has been touted throughout recorded history.

This book of the law shall not depart out of thy
mouth; but shalt meditate therein day and night

that thou mayest observe to do according to all
that is written therein; for then thou shalt make thy
way prosperous, and then thou shalt have good
success.

Joshua 1.8 KJV

Unique Constitution Provides Framework

Recently, the European Union delegates from participating countries have assembled for an anticipated, year-long effort to use the United States Constitution as a framework for designing the European Union's Constitution. Our Constitution provides the necessary checks and balances of power, democratic representation, and allows the unhindered pursuit of personal and economic happiness for its citizens, which they desire to emulate.

As Americans, we tend to take our constitutional liberties and protection for granted. We have allowed our Constitution to be undermined by liberal efforts to transform our society into personal interpretations of nirvana. Yet, our European neighbors, facing a monumentally, historical task of organizing a just and equitable framework for governing the European Union's citizens, chose the United States of America's Constitution, as their inspiration. This alone, should impress the value and wisdom of our Constitution upon the American people.

Chapter 11
Immigration, Wages, And You

Our nation owes much to its immigrants. Undoubtedly, our nation would not exist, at least, in its present form, if it were not for the immigration of millions of people from all over the world. Still, there are pertinent issues affecting the daily lives of many Americans that necessitate our attention, in hopes of initiating debate in search of solutions.

In 1700, there were an estimated 250,000 colonists living in North America, most of them North European settlers. By the time the Declaration of Independence was drafted, declaring our independence from the King of England, an additional 450,000 immigrants had arrived, strengthening our nation's economy and resolve. Roughly, 700,000 European immigrants were responsible for the founding of our nation. Today, not including political refugees, nor family members of American citizens, the United States of America legally accepts 675,000 immigrants each year.

Throughout our nation's history, Americans have been forced to change our immigration policy, based upon existing economic and political conditions. For example, in 1808, after an estimated 375,000 Africans had been imported as slaves, American sentiments forced Congress to make it illegal. Additionally, there were periods when great numbers of immigrants coming to this country, caused Americans to temporarily alter their immigration laws.

During the westward expansion of the mid-1800s, an open immigration policy allowed 7,500,000 immigrants, in hopes of a better life, to legally enter our country. During this time, some states, as well as, railroad companies, openly solicited immigrants for a labor force. Also, when gold was discovered in California in the mid-1800s, Chinese immigrants, with temporary intentions, crossed the Pacific Ocean to try their luck at prospecting for gold.

This great influx of immigrants during the 1800s began to alarm many of the early settlers. During the late 1870s, with fear of job competition lowering wages, Californians demanded excluding Chinese immigrants. In 1882, in addition to the creation of a list of unacceptable immigrants, such as, unaccompanied children, the mentally ill, and indigent, the *Chinese Exclusion Act* was passed by Congress, prohibiting Chinese laborers from immigrating to America.

However, during the next forty years, over 23 million immigrants, from every nation in the world, streamed into this land of opportunity. Again, in fear of reduced wages, and a growing number of impoverished immigrants, Congress passed another law in 1917, requiring adult immigrants to prove they were capable of reading and writing. The law also created the Asiatic Barred Zone, which included most of Asia and the Pacific rim.

Then in 1921, Congress severely limited the total number of immigrants, as well as, limited the number of immigrants from any one nation in an attempt to maintain the *unity* of our country. *The Immigration Act* of 1924, again limited non-Western Hemisphere immigrants to about 154,000 a year.

Obviously, the Great Depression slowed the number of immigrants coming to America for the promise of a better life. During the period between 1931 and 1940, only 500,000 immigrants settled in America. Consequently, due to a lessening of the immigration burden and the outbreak of WWII, immigration policy was again, revised.

This culminated in *The Immigration and Nationality Act*, which was passed in 1952, granting immigration available to those nations that had been previously excluded. Additionally, Congress set separate provisions for political refugees, which opened the door for over 600,000 European and Soviet citizens to escape the devastation of WWII.

In 1965, amendments to the *Immigration and Nationality Act*, favoring relatives, those with special skills and permanent resident aliens, altered patterns of immigration again. In 1978, Congress replaced the 170,000 limit for the Eastern Hemisphere and the 120,000 limit for the Western

Hemisphere with an annual world quota of 290,000. However in 1990, additional amendments to *The Immigration and Nationality Act* of 1952, increased the number of immigrants to 700,000 annually, from 1992 to 1994, and then 675,000 *annually*, beginning in 1995.

Presently, Mexico annually contributes almost 150,000 legal immigrants, three times the number of legal immigrants to this nation, as their closest rival, the Philippines. In addition to Mexico, the major sources of legal immigrants in the Western Hemisphere are Cuba, the Dominican Republic, El Salvador and Jamaica, while the Eastern Hemisphere legal immigrants are primarily from Asia, including the Philippines, China, Vietnam, India, and Russia. Obviously, these numbers only include legal immigration, while illegal immigration numbers remain unknown.

Other countries throughout the world carefully control immigration, depending upon each nation's situation. In the past, some nations have placed discouragingly high entry-taxes upon immigrants from certain countries. Additionally, other countries have implemented careful reviews of each immigrant with strict admittance requirements, favoring certain countries and skills. It does not require an economics degree to understand the negative impact of an extremely liberal immigration policy upon a nation's taxpayers and workers.

As we examine the immigration issue, history illustrates the awareness of Americans, concerning the negative impact of excessive, available workers, contributing to the stagnation of wages, while increasing the taxpayers' burden of providing government services. When the natural dynamics of a supply and demand free enterprise system interact within naturally-occurring parameters, the system balances itself in a gradual, incrementally-evolving process. However, if one of the parameters are continuously affected by external factors, the effects of the natural market forces are thwarted, resulting in either stagnation (low wages) or radical fluctuations (high inflation). Depending on the source, as there are conflicting reports, due to the constant flood of immigrant labor and increased payroll taxes, the average American wage earner has realized a decreased *net* income, while annual gross income has averaged a modest 1.75 % increase over the last twenty years. This is not an incidental result of our liberal immigration policy, but its *purpose*.

According to the *Living Wage Movement's* statistics, the minimum wage is 26 % lower than it was in 1980 (inflation corrected). Recently, National Public Radio (NPR) reported the City of New Orleans, bolstered by the *Living Wage Movement's* efforts, voted a dollar per hour increase to the federal government's minimum wage standard. A citizen of this city was cited as saying: "*The federal minimum wage is not a livable wage; too many of our hotel, restaurant, and other workers are full-time employed, yet living in poverty. This is no longer acceptable.*"

However, a small-business coalition with support consisting of the tourist industry, the local Chamber of Commerce and other businesses, has filed suit in a local court to prevent this wage increase from taking effect. Observers speculate the case will ultimately, be heard in the Louisiana Supreme Court.

As one might observe, we are not pro-business, nor pro-labor. We are conservatively, pro-free enterprise, *without* government interference. A federally-mandated minimum wage might prove unnecessary, if our immigration policy was responsibly managed. Regardless, due to existing circumstances, the citizens of New Orleans have risen up against the federal law and denounced its inequity.

This is a prime example of our federal government's attempts to *fix* self-induced problems, manipulating the free market forces against the wishes of the majority of citizens in the City of New Orleans (liberal *top-down* approach). The citizens of New Orleans have taken a conservative, *bottom-up* approach in their solution: the lowest possible level of government more justly *serves* its citizens.

National Unity

Another problem with our liberal immigration policy is the absence of a common language. Besides the obvious concerns of traffic safety, taxpayer expense, etc., there is a *lack of unity* issue. Why can't Americans learn from the past several millenniums of human history? A nation divided by cultures *and* languages, has not survived. History suggests there must be a unified common thread of *cohesion,* uniting the different cultures of a nation.

Throughout the world's history, empires without a common language, in spite of great efforts to militarily and politically enforce their influences and boundaries, have failed. As an example of this language-barrier motivation for secession, our northern neighbor, Canada, has witnessed recent attempts by the French-speaking minority to seek independence from the majority English-speaking rule.

Additionally, the recent liberal efforts preventing English from being designated as the United States of America's official national language reveals a widespread lack of familiarity with world history, and an admirably, successful effort by liberal, socialist-minded, political reformers. Their efforts *led* uninformed Americans, preventing our nation from unifying, thus weakening our resolve to require immigrants to embrace our nation. Different languages magnify our cultural differences, which only perpetuates the *us vs. them* mentality prevailing in many legal immigrants and the majority of illegal immigrants searching for temporary economic gain at the American citizen's expense.

There is no shame in preserving our nation by demanding immigrants learn our language. *If* they come to our country to integrate into our society, to equally share our nation's liberties, it is advantageous for them to learn English. Is that an exorbitant price to pay for freedom? If they choose to preserve their heritage and continue speaking their native language, that is their privilege. This is America!

Do As I Say, Not As I Do

A disturbing aspect of our government's liberal immigration policies, is the lack of our government's enforcement of existing laws prohibiting undocumented workers. Recently, Wells Fargo Bank began offering illegal immigrants access to mainstream services, accepting cash deposits from undocumented immigrant workers (illegal aliens).

On November 8, 2001, the *Los Angeles Times* reported:

> *Although other banks have quietly begun accepting the cards as well, Wells Fargo, with more than 3,000 branches in 23 states, is the largest institution to adopt their use, and the first bank to publicly promote them. Bank officials said they hope the move will help them tap a lucrative market of consumers who are now outside the mainstream, relying on costly check cashing services and living in a cash economy. "Now immigrants can avoid the worry and risk of keeping their money in the house," John Murillo, a Wells Fargo Bank vice-president, said at the Mexican Consulate in Los Angeles at a news conference aimed at the Spanish-language media. "We welcome you to come to one of our branches, where our Spanish-speaking staff will help you and where we won't question your legal status."*

The article also stated, US Bancorp, Union Bank of California, and credit unions were also quietly accepting the Mexican Consular cards as adequate identification. Additionally, the *Los Angeles Times* article quoted an INS official:

> *Immigration officials did not express concern over the plan. "Our priorities are to go after illegal immigrants involved in committing crime," said Tony Lew, a spokesman for the INS' Los Angeles district office. "If they are law-abiding citizens, we don't have the resources to go looking for them."*

How much more than $2.7 *billion* should it require to have the resources? The INS 2000 fiscal budget included over $2.7 billion strictly for enforcement, with a total budget of over $4.27 billion. It appears that taxpayer money would be better spent if INS agents stood outside banks looking for illegal immigrants, instead of driving their 4X4 SUVs across the hot, desolate California desert.

Additionally, isn't the phrase, *law-abiding citizens*, when applied to illegal immigrants, contradictory on *every* level? First of all, they are NOT citizens. Citizens pay state and federal income taxes, *statutory* citizens and illegal immigrants do not. Secondly, how can *illegal* immigrants be *law-abiding*? Someone is missing the point, could it be us? Are we naive to presume that our government is obligated to enforce the laws of our nation?

The fact that California bankers are publicly challenging our federal government's law enforcement agencies by soliciting illegal banking activities, is undeniable proof of who is *not* in control of our nation. The *Los Angeles Times* continued:

> *This year, the state Senate and Assembly approved a measure that would allow undocumented immigrants who are applying for legal immigration status to obtain a driver's license. The measure was not signed into law, but drew strong backing from immigrant rights groups. The bill is expected to be introduced again next year. Anti-immigrant groups blasted any efforts to serve the undocumented population. "The need for better control over who comes into the country became evident to everybody on Sept. 11," said Ira Mehlman, a spokesman for the Washington-based Federation for American Immigration Reform. "All of these things facilitate these people coming into the country and blending into the scenery. If people are here breaking the law, it shouldn't be the obligation of society to make it more convenient for them."*

The *Los Angeles Times* further states:

> *Banking officials, however, said the immigration status of potential customers is not relevant. And a similar point was made by Orange County law enforcement officials, who have agreed to accept the cards. "Some people seem to think that by doing this, we're supporting illegal immigration. That's not the case," said Laguna Beach Police Chief Jim Spreine, presi-*

*dent of the Orange County Chiefs of Police and
Sheriff's Assn. "The fact is, all the people we serve
should be given equal protection under the law, and
we believe this will help us provide that equal protection."*

Excuse us, last time we checked, law enforcement
agencies serve the citizens and taxpayers within their community, state, or nation. We don't recall any reports of undocumented immigrant workers volunteering a portion of
their tax-free income to help pay for the services which they
receive benefit.

Is it unpatriotic to demand that our government enforce the laws which were passed by our elected representatives? Is it unpatriotic to be concerned about your family,
your livelihood, and your nation? Is that the brush, which
the *Los Angeles Times* was trying to paint the citizens want-
ing to preserve American interests? We are not opposed to
immigration, but we are opposed to hidden agendas by liberal, self-serving, special-interest groups promoting an ex-
cessively, liberal immigration policy and flagrantly, disregarding our nation's laws.

National Public Radio also reported that since the
beginning of this new bank policy, which was approximately
three months previous, Wells Fargo Bank reported opening
1,800 new accounts *daily*, with total cash deposits in excess
of $50 million. This effort, reportedly to lower the incidence
of violence against cash-carrying undocumented workers,
was expected to negatively impact the money wire-transfer
businesses responsible for handling the estimated *$9 billion
per year* being sent back home to Mexico. This new business policy move by California banks is simply an effort to
gain new markets, while flagrantly flaunting their contempt
for our nation's immigration laws.

Obviously, $50 million isn't a *lot* of money, by Cali-
fornia banks or federal government standards, but a 28%
tax-bracket represents $14 million in federal tax revenues.
Certainly, that's not a lot of money, either; but what about
the *untaxed* $9 billion annually sent home to their families?
That same 28% tax bracket would generate over $2.5 bil-

lion dollars per year in additional tax revenues for our federal government. Get the picture? A few billion dollars here, a few billion dollars there... *now* we're starting to talk about real money! That amount would almost pay the federal budget's annual allocation for INS enforcement. Additionally, the negative impact of the loss-of-circulation of $9 billion leaving our economy, instead of creating additional taxable salaries, purchasing commodities, and investing in American enterprises, is staggering.

Immediately, many questions come to mind. First, where are the Immigration and Naturalization Service (INS) employees paid by American taxpayers to detain undocumented workers? What about enforcing the penalties for those employers hiring them? If our INS is not going to obey the laws, are all Americans able to choose which laws they obey? If our government's *only* source of power is that which is *granted* by its citizens, then logically, we *must* own the same rights to disobey the laws of this nation.

Finally, *how* is the Internal Revenue Service going to collect taxes from noncitizen depositors without a social security number? The *Los Angeles Times* reported:

> *If they have neither, (social security or federal ID) however, they can open bank accounts by signing an Internal Revenue Service form for nonresident immigrants that puts their home address on file with the IRS... Banks are not compelled to ask for Social Security numbers, but they must abide by IRS and federal Bank Secrecy Act regulations.*

Are illegal aliens *undocumented* immigrants or *nonresident* immigrants? Is their home address in Mexico? Is this a double standard? Have *you* ever tried to open a bank account without providing either a social security number or Federal ID? It is *NOT* going to happen! Unless, you're an undocumented worker with *superior* rights, and no financial income tax burden. Additionally, we are certain the banks will verify these addresses as true and correct before opening an account, as well.

Is the IRS going to ignore these untaxed wage earnings, of which the deposits are proof? Does that mean we can eliminate the INS and save $4.27 billion annually? Will Americans claim Mexican citizenship, but choose to remain illegally in the United States, avoiding federal income taxes?

These recent events undermine the United States of America's efforts to protect our borders and responsibly manage an already, excessively-liberal immigration policy. Why aren't the INS, IRS, and the American people protesting this action? Hello?!? Is *anybody* home? Are we missing something here? Perhaps our mainstream media, our *watchdogs* of justice, are conveniently snoozing on the front porch under the legs of an aged and weakened Uncle Sam, snoring in his rocker.

We don't blame illegal immigrants. Again, we blame ourselves, for *allowing* our government's hypocritical stance on the enforcement of *our* laws, which *our* duly elected representatives have passed. It serves no good purpose to harbor resentment towards others, only by accepting responsibility for our actions, or inactions, can we progress.

As Dr. Wayne Dyer, Ph.D., author of the *New York Times* best-seller *Erroneous Zones*, and former graduate studies professor at St. John's University in New York, is fond of stating:

> *You can't solve a problem with the same mind that created it.*

We must change our nation's priorities, attitude, and path, otherwise, we leave our children an uncertain future.

A return to conservative values is necessary to protect the American citizens and this nation, which we cherish. Unfortunately, this downward trend in *net* real wages and economic opportunity is not going to correct *itself*. We will be required to force our government to address these issues by our action at the polls. Only when you become informed, involved, and a participant in our political process will there be a difference. Otherwise, remember that our government is designed to serve those that *do* participate, and unquestionably, corporate America is an *active* participant.

Chapter 12
What *Do* We Know?

Have you ever channel-surfed through the news media outlets and found it peculiar that there are three hundred million Americans, fifty states, several U.S. territories, an abundance of domestic and foreign issues, and basically, the same news stories are on *every* channel? Surely, it is no surprise to know that our mainstream media is owned and directed by the same principals that lobby our Congress for economic benefits at taxpayer expense? Would you find it difficult to imagine that these individuals affect the news presented to the American people, either protecting or furthering their own personal interests?

In recent years, there have been countless disclosures by disgruntled reporters and alienated news commentators that have substantiated this concern. But, don't expect the mainstream media to become alarmed or focused on this issue, as they are too busy reporting the *acceptable* news. As a possible alternative, public radio and television, as well as, independent publishers, are good sources for a broader and more objective review of national and world issues. Still, each citizen must rely upon their own judgment to gather an opinion about the matter, independent of any opinions or insinuations, expressed in the presentation.

Currently, there are two best-sellers on the market, which address this very issue. The first, by Bernard Goldberg, *Bias*, documents liberal, politically-correct stories reported by network news, as lacking substantive, factual basis. *Bias* targets news reports on a wide-array of contemporary societal woes, from the *supposed* teenage HIV epidemic to the coverage of President Clinton *solving* the middle-class, blonde, blue-eyed, homeless crisis. Goldberg promotes truthful reporting on real issues, in lieu of, pursuing viewer-rating scores.

The second book, William McGowan's *Coloring the News*, approaches the issue from a different perspective. McGowan describes a liberal agenda being promoted within the newsroom by a sensitivity to offensive topics. He documents two contrasting stories affecting homosexuality, one in which, Matthew Shepherd, a homosexual, is a murder victim. The Matthew Shepherd story was covered by the major networks, and widely reported in over 3,000 stories worldwide. The other story, less politically-correct, received only local news coverage. It is the story of Jesse Dirkhising, a 13 year old Arkansas boy who was gagged, tied down, raped and left to slowly suffocate, by two homosexuals living next door.

Both of these crimes were horrendous acts committed by calloused, cruel individuals, and deserving of national news coverage. However, when McGowan pressed the *Los Angeles Times*, and the major networks on why the great disparity between coverage, the typical response was: "The Dirkhising case was only *local* news".

The majority of our news media is owned and controlled by less than a dozen different entities. For various reasons, much of our nation's news is censored, filtered, or reported with prejudice. If Americans perceive major network news organizations as striving to protect their personal interests and rely *solely* upon them as a source of enlightened, objective news coverage, disregarding the *accuracy* issue, they are only glimpsing a minute fraction of the issues affecting them. Unlike the great American, Paul Harvey: "*In a moment... the rest of the story*", we are short-changed.

A Government Tool

As a nation, our attention is continuously distracted by the pushing of our emotional *hot* buttons, creating an illusion of information on the *official* issues of our society. A world of sixty-second sound bytes requires many difficult decisions on news worthiness; however, political leaders utilize the society-shaping power of the news media broadcasts to manipulate public-opinion, promoting personal political agendas. Although major news networks *do* provide a beneficial tool for our government to communicate its intentions, actions, and reactions to domestic and global issues, Americans must realize our federal government's news releases are carefully planned, screened and presented.

On February 23, 1967, political scholar Noam Chomsky's *The Responsibility of Intellectuals* was printed in the *New York Review*:

> *When Arthur Schlesinger was asked by The New York Times in November, 1965, to explain the contradiction between his published account of the Bay of Pigs incident and the story he had given the press at the time of the attack, he simply remarked that he had lied; and a few days later, he went on to compliment the Times for also having suppressed information on the planned invasion, in "the national interest," as this term was defined by the group of arrogant and deluded men of whom Schlesinger gives such a flattering portrait in his recent account of the Kennedy Administration. It is of no particular interest that one man is quite happy to lie in behalf of a cause which he knows to be unjust; but it is significant that such events provoke so little response in the intellectual community — for example, no one has said that there is something strange in the offer of a major chair in the humanities to a historian who feels it to be his duty to persuade the world that an American-sponsored invasion of a nearby country is nothing of the sort. And what of the incredible sequence of lies on the part of our government and its spokesmen concerning such matters as negotiations in Vietnam? The facts are known to all who care to know. The press, foreign and domestic, has presented documentation to refute each falsehood as it appears. But the power of the government's propaganda apparatus is such that the citizen who does not undertake a research project on the subject can hardly hope to confront government pronouncements with fact.*

We are continuously bombarded with the *official* news. One cannot listen to the radio, watch television, or read the newspapers, without the last minute update on the Israeli-Palestinian conflict, the *War on Terrorism,* or planned American aggression against Iraq, Korea, or some other nation. What about American lives, rising unemployment, rampant crime, soaring health care costs, and obsolete job skills? Must we focus on the world's problems?

Obviously, our news media is fully-supportive of the current administration's focus on internationalism. Perhaps sensational military clips increase viewer ratings, but we *must* examine the plight of Americans. In order to force political solutions, Americans must demand our media *spotlight* critical domestic issues, as well. We should lead the world by protecting Americans' living standards, creating a robust economy, and safeguarding our freedoms. A defense industry economy is not in our best national interests. Let's export goods and goodwill, instead of war and ill-will.

As we attempt to overcome the negativity of political inaction by encouraging the American citizens to regain control of their nation's government by wrestling it away from the clutches of the minority, we expect and quite frankly, hope for a response from those advocates of the status quo, similar to that which Tom Wolfe described in a letter to *New York Magazine* on April 25, 1968:

> *Its followers - marvelous! - react just like those of*
> *any other totem group when somebody suggests that*
> *their holy buffalo knuckle may not be holy after all.*
> *They scream like weenies over a wood fire!!*

We are not conspiracy theorists, nor are we attempting to malign any individuals. We are certain that the liberal policies that are being pursued, for the most part, are perceived by their advocates as manipulating the *system* with no harmful effect upon our nation. However, any manipulation or withholding of the truth, regardless of motivation, inflicts damage on a free and open society. *We the People* cannot properly oversee government, if we are not presented the *actual* facts in their *entirety.*

142

Who *is* making the decisions?

Knowledge is power, right? A *possibly*, unorganized group of highly-educated, financially-empowered intellectuals, in conjunction with our nation's political leaders, use their extensive resources and practical understanding of the mechanics of our nation's political system to preserve the status quo, furthering their own personal interests, while mounting perceived public-opinion, confounding attacks on any opponents *daring* to challenge their self-serving, liberal agenda. Using mass media to shape public opinion, many of our nation's political and business leaders strive to supplant original thought with their contrived perspectives, thus, affording them continued pursuit of their personal agendas, unknown to the majority of unsuspecting Americans.

Unfortunately, most Americans are too distracted earning a living and raising a family to feel informed enough to challenge or even question the validity of these liberal positions. The power of mass media is not fathomable by the average American. Under the guise of entertainment and objective news coverage, calculated subliminal and indirect persuasions affect the minds of viewers. The entire industry is *for-profit* and *self-serving*, but somehow, the majority of Americans have been deluded to believing their purpose is philanthropic, in nature. America must become a freethinking society, again. Are we going to continue allowing an elite few to restrict our nation's political topics to the issues, which they choose?

We realize we are *preaching to the choir*, because you have already made the investment to buy this book and read it. However, the question remains, will you take political action? Will you recommend this book, or other similar books, to motivate a friend into action? Will you participate in your nation's political process and vote? Will you encourage your family and friends to participate, also? We are not attempting to dissuade your personal feelings and interests. We only hope to present the evidence and encourage our readers to openly express their *personal* opinions on the issues and candidates, by taking action... and voting! Only then will you know, firsthand, *who* is making the decisions.

Chapter 13

Tough Love

We write this book, not to destructively criticize our nation, its leaders, or the American citizens, but to contribute to the perpetuation of the personal and economic freedoms provided to all Americans by the greatest nation on earth, the United States of America. As a final quote from the imprisoned Dr. Martin Luther King Jr.:

> *If I have said anything in this letter that is an overstatement of the truth and is indicative of an unreasonable impatience, I beg you to forgive me. If I have said anything in this letter that is an understatement of the truth and is indicative of my having a patience that makes me patient with anything less than brotherhood, I beg God to forgive me.*

We realize that the average citizen is overwhelmed by the hectic pace of American society. However, this fact alone, argues a necessary change in the direction of our culture. Humanity is destined for an existence which allows us to reap the benefits of our efforts, yet still have time to enjoy everyday life. We must practice constraint to counter the natural human desire for the accumulation of material comforts. When our lives on this earth are in the winter of their existence, as we reflect upon the choices we made, the pursuits of our lifetime, and the priorities we chose, will our material luxuries or possessions even be considered?

God created humanity to aspire to the most dignified existence possible. It is for this reason that each of us must strive to safeguard our inheritance to convey it intact to our children. Leonardo da Vinci's enthrallment with the flight of birds allowed him to observe the following:

> *A mother goldfinch, seeing her children caged, feeds them a bit of a poisonous plant, noting, "Better death than to be without freedom".*

Likewise, our great American patriot, the Virginian Patrick Henry, in the closing statements of his historical speech addressed to the Virginia Provincial Convention, delivered exactly 227 years ago on this very day, March 23, 1775:

> *Why stand we here idle? What is it that gentlemen wish? What would they have? Is life so dear, or peace so sweet, as to be purchased at the price of chains and slavery? Forbid it, Almighty God! I know not what course others may take; but as for me, give me liberty or give me death!*

These great men understood the value of freedom, shared their thoughts for humanity's benefit, and lived their lives, accordingly. Neither hesitated a moment, to consider life without liberty, more disconcerting than no life at all. Fortunately, Americans are not required to choose between life and liberty... yet. However, our time of leisurely neglect for our nation's future is gone. The American people's patriotic responsibility to preserve our heritage has never been more critical than today. The unseen enemies: greed, corruption, and despair, are no less threatening to our freedom than terrorism or the world's greatest armies.

Perhaps our dream of an America without poverty, violence, and desperation, will never be realized. Again, the great American philosopher, Dr. Reinhold Niebuhr, in his book *Moral Man and Immoral Society*:

> *Human society will never escape the problem of the equitable distribution of the physical and cultural goods which provide for the preservation and fulfillment of human life... and it may be that there will be no salvation for the human spirit from the more and*

*more painful burdens of social injustice until the
ominous tendency in human history has resulted in
perfect tragedy.*

However, if *every* American's equal right to pursue
happiness is protected from the onslaught of unjust government intrusion, corporate pilfering, and the domestic and
foreign threats of violence, then every patriot in America
can be proud of their efforts. Our nation's citizens have en-
trusted our federal government with no greater responsibility than to preserve this most precious human right. While
the states are capable of administering to the poor, the invalid, and the widowed without the additional burden of a
federal bureaucracy's oversight and expense, our federal
government alone, is in the unique position of both facilitating and enforcing this noble, egalitarian mandate.

The limited scope concept of our federal government
was not a foolish, whimsical dream of our founding fathers,
but a critical design requirement, which was patterned after
the great historical self-governing documents and institutions of the world. Their wisdom has withstood the ages
from intellectual scrutiny, the benefits of hindsight, and the
natural laws of the Creator, which govern the universe. Is it
not foolish for modern Americans, with such little regard
and in hopes of possible easy quick-fixes, to *dismantle* the
time-tested, proven legacy which we have inherited?

Our nation's political leaders have abandoned logic,
common sense, accountability, and American patriotism. We
must become lifetime students of our nation's history, our
government, free enterprise, and our free society. Our most
wasted resource is our God-given human intelligence. It is
no secret that the human brain capacity is drastically, under-
utilized. We must *better* utilize this great gift that was be-
stowed upon us. Leonardo da Vinci wrote:

*For in truth, great love is born of great knowledge of
the thing loved.*

Will we gain the love for our nation that is necessary for us
to take action to save it?

146

The opportunity for Americans to reach out, grasp the hand of freedom, and secure its survival for future generations is fading quickly. We believe that Americans *do* care about their personal freedoms. We believe Americans *do* want to continue to protect our liberty against those forces which threaten its promise of happiness and prosperity. This is our justification for exposing ourselves to the threats of opposition, censure, and possible harm. We love our nation enough to put ourselves on the line, do **YOU**?

Where will each of us stand in the *courtroom* of the Universe? Will we stand alongside the accused? Or will we stand on the side of justice with a moral conscience intact, knowing we chose to affect a difference? There are no fatalistic concerns about our nation's future survival, that are undeserved. If we allow our egos to deceive ourselves, pretend that we are exempt from the lessons of history, that the ancient sins of mankind will not reduce our nation into oblivion, unless we counter this path of least resistance with our individual efforts, then we deserve our fate.

Samuel Adams, in his speech to the Philadelphia State House on August 1, 1776, stated:

> *If ye love wealth better than liberty, the tranquility of servitude better than the animating contest of freedom, go home from us in peace. We ask not your counsels or arms. Crouch down and lick the hands which feed you. May your chains set lightly upon you, and may posterity forget that ye were our countrymen.*

As our planet's gravity exerts its force on the physical world, limiting its heights, the natural forces of destruction exert their forces upon a nation of people striving to rise above the sins and temptations of humanity. We must not allow our great nation to falter, crumble to ruin, and fall prey to the predators of liberty. Each of us *equally* share in the pleasures and privileges of freedom; likewise, each of us *equally* share the responsibility for its protection. Please accept *your* responsibility, if not for yourself, for your children.   THE END.

147

Call To Arms

Expressions of emotions cloud our consciousness,
Smothering our perceptions with layers of confusion.
Our heart alone remains above the fray,
Waiting patiently to guide our way.

Yearning for tomorrow, dreaming of yesterday,
Glazes the present, as if it were clay.
Open your mind, exhale your doubts,
Let your inner-self, with society bout.

Are not we all made in God's likeness,
Divinity in ungilded splendor?
Know you are unique, know you are Divine,
For no other has your exact same mind.

Take time to ponder, to reflect upon your life,
To control our own destiny, we must always strive.
Accepting nothing without question, trusting only your soul
Is humanity's duty and task for which to toil.

Farah Bazzrea

Bibliography

The World Book Encylopedia, World Book, Inc., 2001

Dr. Henry H. Halley, *Halley's Bible Handbook,* Zondervan Publishing House, 2000

Michael J. Gelb, *How to Think like Leonardo da Vinci,* Dell Publishing, 1998

Ronald Reagan, *An American Life, Ronald Reagan, The Autobiography,* Simon and Schuster, 1990

Billy Graham, *Just As I Am,* Guideposts, 1997

James T. Evans, *Where Liberals Go To Die*, Commonwealth Publishing, 1994

Ideas On Liberty, Foundation For Economic Education, June 2001 - Fredric Bastiat

The Holy Bible, KJV, The World Publishing Company, NY, 1913

One Nation Under God, Barbour Publishing, Inc., 2001

Http://www.mises.org/fredericbastiat.asp - Fredric Bastiat

Http://www.access.gpo.gov/su_docs/aces/aces150.html - *The Congressional Record*

Http://www.cigaraficionado.com/Cigar/Aficionado/people/fc995.html - Dr. Arthur M. Schlesinger, Jr.

Http://www.english.upenn.edu/~afilreis/50s/schleslib.html - Dr. Arthur M. Schlesinger, Jr.

Http://www.drwaynedyer.com/ - Dr. Wayne Dyer

Http://freedomsite.net/93-549.htm - 93d Congress Senate Report No. 93-549, 1st Session

Http://www.barefootsworld.net/war_ep1.html - Senate Report No. 93-549, 1st Session

Http://www.calneva.com/money/lawsuit3.htm - President Roosevelt/Executive Orders 6073, 6102, 6111, & 6260

Http://odur.let.rug.nl/~usa/P/aj7/about/bio/jackxx.htm - President Andrew Jackson

Http://members.tripod.com/~jtlawson/ - Louisiana Purchase

Http://members.aol.com/poesgirl/12919.htm - President Bill Clinton's Executive Order No. 12919

Http://www.disastercenter.com/laworder/12919.htm - President Bill Clinton's Executive Order No. 12919

Http://www.apfn.org/apfn/1933.htm - Trading With The Enemy Act

Http://www.barefootsworld.net/war_ep.html - War and Emergency Powers Acts

Http://dailynews.yahoo.com/full_coverage/us/presidential_elections_2000 - Presidential Election 2000

Http://thomas.loc.gov/r102/r102h04my2.html - Rep. Henry B. Gonzalez (*National And International Thievery In High Places*)

Http://www.npr.org/ - U.S. supplied Afghan textbooks

Http://www.stanford.edu/group/King/ - Dr. Martin Luther King, Jr.

Http://www.fas.umontreal.ca/HST/hst7000/ShapiroPC.htm - Ellen Schrecker (Politically-correct education)

Http://cbc.ca/cgi-bin/templates/view.cgi?/news/2001/08/21/lumber010821 - Prime Minister Chretien/Lumber Tariff

Http://www.rjrt.com/TI/Pages/TITaxesLegisCigTaxSum.asp - RJ Reynolds/Tobacco Tax

Http://www.prfaa.com/eng/index.asp - Puerto Rico

Http://www.oznet.net/cyrus/cyrus_g.htm - Cyrus The Great

Http://www.gpo.gov/nara/nara001.html - National Archives and Records Administration

Http://www.cato.org/pubs/ssps/ssp1.html - Social Security

Http://www.religion-online.org/ - Reinhold Niebuhr

Http://www.wwy.org/wwy2795.html - America's Noble Heritage - Grover Cleveland Quote

Http://www.pananet.com/pancanal/pcc.htm - Panama Canal

Http://www.eia.doe.gov/emeu/cabs/panama.html - Panama Canal

Http://www.capitalism.net/excerpts/exc_014.htm - Wages

Http://www.inquiria.com/keynes/gt/app3.htm - Wages

Http://www.epinet.org/webfeatures/viewpoints/LW_movement.html - Wages

Http://www.hal-pc.org/~clyndes/political-chomsky.html - Noam Chomsky

Http://www.coloringthenews.com/html/feature_cov_bglobe.html - *Bias* and *Coloring the News*

Http://www.priweb.com/internetlawlib/89.htm - Int'l. Law

We want to hear from you. If you have any questions, or comments, please contact us at the following:

Proverbial Publishing Co.
125 N. Trade St.
Shelby, NC 28150

Ph. (704) 487-7323
Fx. (704) 487-8262
Email: Pubbooks@bellsouth.net

For content errors, omissions, or discussion, please contact the listed author per the following:

Farah Bazzrea - Email: farah_bazzrea@hotmail.com